S0-AUR-257

The Wit & Wisdom of
Richard Needham

Richard J. Needham

The Wit & Wisdom of
Richard Needham

Illustrations by Ed Franklin

Hurtig Publishers
Edmonton

Copyright © 1977 by Richard J. Needham

No part of this book may be reproduced
or transmitted in any form by any means,
electric or mechanical, including
photocopying and recording, or by any
information storage or retrieval
system, without written permission from
the publisher, except for brief
passages quoted by a reviewer in
a newspaper or magazine.

Hurtig Publishers
10560 105 Street
Edmonton, Alberta

ISBN 0-88830-137-5 clothbound
ISBN 0-88830-138-3 paperback

Printed and bound in Canada

Contents

To Richard S. Malone

Introduction

RICHARD JOHN NEEDHAM is a man of medium proportions. He is neither tall nor short, fat nor thin. His hair is neither thick nor sparse, grey nor white. His posture is neither good nor bad; his gait is neither springy nor sprung. He is neither jolly nor morose; he is neither young nor old. He makes a reasonable contribution to the crowds in which other people stand out.

He is a progressive thinker held captive by eternal verities, a Don Quixote who respects windmills, a man from Walden who would perish beyond the city's gates. Somerset Maugham could have used him as the archetypal civil servant. That would have been very bad casting indeed. He would befuddle any bureaucracy to which he was attached.

In another time, he might have been in the quality control division of the firm that built the pyramids. He might have polished lamps for Diogenes or supervised the simultaneous translation devices for the committee in charge of the King James version. Today the talent for being accessory to splendid undertakings is hived in newspaper offices. In these places, a man flourishes without commitment to the enterprises which engage him or responsibility for their results. To write well and wisely of the building of the Canadian Pacific Railway or the sinking of the Titanic is the same thing.

It is a vanity of the day (nourished, no doubt, by schools of journalism) to refer to such writers as members of the newspaper profession. They are no such thing. Neither are they members of a craft. There is no prescribed period or range of instruction that precedes the earning of a living in this business. There are no examinations which must be passed, no certificates which must be issued, no formal apprenticeships which must be served, no tools with which a man must be proficient before he can persuade an editor to print his stuff. Newspaper work, like the lesser callings that flow from it, is day labour. The people who are good at it are good day labourers. The people who are not good at it, whatever degrees, licences, and honours they may possess, are not good day labourers. They should avoid ditches.

Within the limits set down, Richard Needham was superbly qualified when he was hired onto his first newspaper in 1930. His curriculum vitae then included half of the material to be found in his biographical file at *The Globe and Mail* today. Born in Gibraltar . . . lost his father in the First World War . . . emigrated to Canada . . . bound to win.

The somewhat loose educational requirements for the newspaper business may be an advantage when entering it. They contribute nothing to survival afterward. Needham survived by acquiring an encyclopedic knowledge of his new country (including both of its official languages) and of the world context in which Canada functioned. By becoming an oracle in such matters as constitutional history, western freight rates, Great Lakes water levels, Keynesian economics and international liquidity, he hacked his way onto his first editorial board where he was paid, not just to record day to day history, but also to say what was thought about it – what his editor thought about it and sometimes, deliciously, what he thought about it himself.

That, of course, is the Holy Grail of the accessories business: the opportunity to write about something in such a way that what was written may be recalled after the something itself has been forgotten. The inevitable leap here is from editorial writer to columnist – from the arguments and pronouncements of the collectivity to the sweet reasoning of personal observation.

Needham's daily column in *The Globe and Mail* (it has never had any other title) began without a byline and without any particular purpose other than to open windows to wit and, occasionally, fantasy. He assaulted his space like a wave of camp followers in hot pursuit of an army: fairy tales, love letters, advice to the lovelorn, valentines, quotations, essays, sermons, encyclicals. He offered contests and puzzles and, when they were still illegal, conducted lotteries (with school principals making the lucky draws). The Needham coffee klatches drew hundreds of teenagers. Younger kids joined his discovery trips to the outports of Newfoundland. He went on speaking tours and gave away roses in public libraries.

And, over the years, he increasingly built his own case against the directions in which Canadian society was moving. In Needham's heaven – or hell – most of the schools would be closed, children would be off their parents' backs and into their own adventures at age sixteen at the latest, violence would be punished as the greatest sin (with paddle and rope restored), politics would be purged from the right, men would be restored to the company of women, and heavenly hosts would provide the new Musak from the Anglican hymnary. All of these causes are served with priestly vocation, sometimes in lengthy series of columns, sometimes in single paragraphs in his notebooks.

Increasingly, his space and energies have been consumed by his conservatism. When Needham advised his readers not to vote for any of the present crop of politicians, his newspaper shot back: "He is Vesuvius erupting, the Red River in flood, the Poseidon upside down and sinking."

At his typewriter, Needham is never the man of medium proportions.

Introducing him at a Leacock awards dinner years ago, I described him as a Mona Lisa in need of a shave. I probably offended him. I should have recognized God reaching down from the roof of the Sistine Chapel.

Richard J. Doyle

Friends & Lovers

If there is one, just one, person in your life who never hassles you, congratulations, you've got it made.

One of life's most difficult tasks is to write a character reference for someone you know.

One's friends are like one's books – some hardcover, but mainly paperbacks.

Practically all of us pretend to be concerned with the poverty problem or the pollution problem or the Quebec problem or some other damn problem. And maybe we are, but that isn't what is on the top of our minds. What is bugging every one of us is our relationship or non-relationship with one other human being – with our father, mother, husband, wife, son, daughter, brother, sister, sweetheart, whatever. Human relationships are the problem; if they bring us much of the joy we get in life, they bring us practically all of the misery. That is why, as I grow older, I am becoming something of a recluse – liking a few people, but keeping them at a distance.

Everybody talks about brotherly love; history and literature have something to tell us about brotherly hate.

Brotherhood – ah yes, and how well did you get along with your own brothers?

A good friend is one who accepts your lies in as calm and good-natured a fashion as you accept his. Or hers.

What are you really like? Your friends know. They won't tell you – they are, after all, your friends – but they know.

I suspect that in every relationship, however warm and affectionate, there is an element of hostility – a lurking, atavistic desire to put the other person down, to place him or her in the wrong, to make him or her feel guilty. If we were wise, we would recognize this and accept it and be amused by it. An element of rivalry – of swordplay as it were – perhaps goes along with love, as the thorn goes along with the rose, the bone with the kipper.

There was once a hermit who lived in a hollow tree and took confessions. A man came along saying, "My name is Arthur and I'm crazy about a woman named Beatrice, but she pays no attention to me." He was followed by a woman who said, "My name is Beatrice and I'm crazy about a man named Charles, but he pays no attention to me." Next came a man who said, "My name is Charles and I'm crazy about a woman named Dorothy, but she pays no attention to me." After him came a woman who said, "My name is Dorothy and I'm crazy about a man named Arthur, but he pays no attention to me." At this point, the hermit sighed heavily, slammed down his grille, and poured himself a stiff drink.

Caution in love? No! That's like eating a hard-boiled egg with the shell still on it.

A woman enjoys being loved by a wise man, providing he does it foolishly.

A woman gets her life neatly organized, then waits hopefully for some man to come along and knock it sideways.

There isn't much point in sending a love letter these days. By the time she gets it, she will have met and married someone else.

I heard about a young man whose love life was unsatisfactory, so he went to the store and saw a book called *How to Hug* and bought it and took it home triumphantly and found it to be the eighth volume of an encyclopedia.

My mother always said that the test of true love was whether you would use his (her) toothbrush.

Love is never having to say you are sorry; it shows from the look on your face.

Most of us go through life looking for the right person and sometimes thinking we have found him or her and then getting upset because he or she doesn't turn out to be the right person after all. This is rather like looking for the Kingdom of Heaven which, as Jesus said, is inside you – there or nowhere at all. The right person can only be found within you; make yourself right, and your relationships will look after themselves.

Every relationship we have with another person is rather less, or rather more, than we would like it to be.

Those who recognize the importance of being together also recognize the importance of being apart. Like day and night, like food and hunger, like sin and sanctity, the two need one another.

Men and women generally see too much of each other; as a result, they get bored and take each other for granted. I think a man and a woman should come together as if each had returned from a long journey and was preparing to depart on another.

I imagine that for every affair caused by physical desire, there are one hundred caused by curiosity, or boredom, or both.

People, especially young people, get annoyed when I tell them there is no way to understand another human being. They think that in ruling out understanding, I am ruling out love, friendship, etc. Not at all. I don't understand how the presses work at *The Globe and Mail*, but I love to watch and hear them. I adore Bach's Toccata and Fugue in D Minor, but I can't tell you why. Mystery – the lack of understanding – seems to me an essential ingredient of humanity and human relationships, especially those between men and women.

When love comes in the door, truth flies out the window. And vice versa.

Lying and love go together. The more people you love, the more people who love you, the more you will lie and be lied to. It is the unpopular person who can afford to tell the truth. Maybe that is what makes him unpopular?

Most people lie in bed, but an occasional one tells the truth.

Love is never having to say you are sorry. It is placing other people in the position where they constantly have to say that *they* are sorry.

It is better to be hated than to be loved. When you are hated, you know precisely where you are at. You are also treated much more politely.

Make the world a better place; treat the people you love with the same civility as you treat the people you detest.

Of course, they aren't in love; haven't you noticed how polite they are to each other?

There is the one who loves the more, and there is the one who loves the less, and you know which one is always in command.

Promises are no doubt sincere at the moment they are made, but with the passage of time the sincerity tends to evaporate. I think all promises should be date-stamped like a bus transfer, valid only if used within a certain period. Thus, a promise to take her to dinner might be deemed to expire after two weeks; a promise to love her eternally and exclusively, after two days.

"Why can't this night go on forever?" If it did, my romantic friend, you would be the very first to complain.

If people didn't promise to love each other forever, they might love each other just a little bit longer than they do.

Affairs of the heart are very nice, to be sure, but affairs of the head last longer.

Every quarrel damages a relationship which, in most cases, is worth far more than the word or deed that brought on the quarrel.

A love affair which can survive the lending and borrowing of money can survive anything.

It is amazing how much free time a man has when he falls in love with a woman and how little he has when he gets over it.

A truly great love affair doesn't fade away; it drops dead.

A fellow I know was driving me down to work, and we got talking about the possibility of friendship – just plain, simple friendship – between men and women. He said, "I think a woman can manage it, but not a man, he'd have sex in his mind." I replied, "Now, Jack, I very much like your wife Betty, and she sometimes comes down to have lunch with me, but I certainly don't desire her." He replied tartly, "Why not? Is there something wrong with her?" and the rest of the ride was quite frosty.

In everybody's life, sex begins as a mystery which turns into a melodrama which turns into a tragedy which turns into a farce.

There are two things you should never do from a sense of duty, and the other one is to read a book.

A wise woman told me, "Love is the building; sex is the penthouse you finally construct on the top. Where we make a mistake is in constructing the penthouse first, then trying to put up the building beneath it."

Men offer love in the hope of getting sex; women offer sex in the hope of getting love; both are cheated.

The permissive society is a bore. It's no fun breaking the rules when there aren't any.

Don't take her out to dinner and tell her she is sexy and attractive. Take her out to lunch and tell it to her; that way, she knows there isn't any angle.

They should put the Gideon Bible in the hotel lobby, not in the hotel bedroom; by the time you get to the bedroom, it's too late.

I used to think that if we brought sex completely into the open, people would switch their minds over to something else. Well anyway, that is what I used to think.

When a girl says, "I want you to meet my friend, he's a really beautiful person," I steel myself to encounter something that looks and acts as if it just escaped from the zoo.

When you give, forget about it and allow the receiver to forget about it, too – as in any case he or she will.

I agree with La Rochefoucauld (and it is certainly true in my case) that what appears to be a kind or generous action almost always has selfish motives – to buy the friendship or loyalty of the person helped, or to make the giver feel good, or get him into Heaven. It follows from this that if people were more selfish, they would do more nice things for others, and that is my program for improving the world.

After visiting your friendly neighbourhood supermarket, you wonder what the hostile ones must be like.

Simply to be yourself, simply to live your own life, you must fight one hundred battles every day – not with your enemies, but with your friends, not with those who don't love you, but with those who do.

Don't annoy your friends by lying to them; tell the truth and get rid of them completely.

Spend twenty-four hours with another person, and you will have ample cause to like or dislike him, admire or despise him, love or hate him. It depends on what you yourself want; he will give you all the reasons you need.

There are three or four people in my life with whom I get along pretty well – not because I understand them, but because I don't and don't specially want to; not because they understand me, but because they don't and don't specially want to – and I don't specially want them to either. Isn't that what Santayana had in mind when he said people are friends in spots?

In our relationships with other people, we commonly pay a dollar's worth of misery to get a dime's worth of happiness.

A man is in trouble according to the number of people who are close to him and according to the degree of that closeness.

Many people have told me they were fed up with their friends, but nobody ever told me he was fed up with his enemies.

Fair competition is when you undercut the other guy; unfair competition is when he undercuts you.

One sure way to reduce the amount of suffering in this world is to be silent about your own.

When a man tells me about all the injustices he has suffered, I begin to understand why they have been inflicted on him. Indeed, by the time he is finished, I am ready to inflict a few on him myself.

Our friends have excellent taste in liking us; they have very strange taste in the other people they like.

We like our friends, but it is rarely we like our friends' friends.

You may like him, or you may like her, but you hardly ever like both of them.

When you go to someone's home for dinner, take an alarm clock set to go off at 10:00 P.M. You will be relieved to hear it ring; so will they.

Some day I will be brave enough to tell a hostess, "I don't want a drink before dinner; I want dinner."

If you invite someone to your home, they will probably stay on and on, with you anxious to get rid of them, and if you accept an invitation to someone's home, you will be expected to stay on and on, meanwhile wishing you could get away. A good way around this is to entertain people (and let them entertain you) in restaurants – one hour, two at most, and you are free, free, free.

We drop our friends not because they have ceased to amuse us but because we have ceased to amuse them. A new and more appreciative audience is required.

If you are fond of someone, you can't be annoyed by anything they do or say; it is when the fondness wears off that you start picking on them. In January, a man will patiently wait half an hour for a woman and joke about it when she turns up. In July, the same man will blow his stack at the same woman for being five minutes late.

We are willing to let a meal end, to let a book or play or movie end, to let a day end, even to let a life end. Why, then, are we so upset over the ending of a friendship, a love, a marriage? Isn't it largely a matter of wounded vanity – a finding out that we were not, after all, indispensable? We would do better to say of it, as we must say of everything else, that it was great while it lasted. Thanks for the memory!

Your friends are drifting off, and that is okay with you; you have discovered they are a bunch of boring old frauds. But stay, just why are they drifting off? Is it possible (don't flinch, bite the bullet), is it possible they have discovered you yourself are a boring old fraud?

One of the surest ways to break up a relationship is by telling the other person your innermost secrets. You will eventually forgive yourself for the telling, but you will never forgive him or her for the listening, for the knowing.

Two people you will always avoid – the one to whom, in your hour of need, you turned for help, and the one to whom, in your hour of grief, you told all.

You eventually forgive the people you helped, but you will never forgive the people who helped you.

Gratitude – the warm feeling you have toward someone who has helped you during the last twenty-four hours.

It costs to give presents, but it costs even more to get them. When you give, you know what the price is; when you get, you don't know; the bill comes along later.

Do a fellow a kindness and he will forget it in twenty-four hours; do him an injury and he will remember it for twenty-four years.

We love the man who promises to help us, tolerate him while he does it, and hate him when he stops doing it.

A man's loyalty doesn't depend on what you have done for him in the past, but on what you have the power to do for him (or to him) in the future. When your ability to help (or hurt) other people disappears, they, too, tend to disappear.

There is less ingratitude in the world than you think because there is less generosity than you think.

Politics & the World

I heard about an old lady who was asked on election day how she had voted. She tartly replied, "I never vote; it only encourages them."

The way I see it, everybody is running the show except the people elected or appointed to run the show.

Government of the people, by the people, for the people, usually ends up as government of the people, by the government, for the government.

A fool thinks that the world is governed by the right people; a sensible man thinks it is governed by clowns, knaves, and psychopaths; a wise man thinks it is governed by the right people, that is to say, clowns, knaves, and psychopaths.

Three statements which nobody, but nobody, believes: (1) The cheque is in the mail, (2) Of course, I will respect you as much in the morning, and (3) I'm from the government and I've come to help you.

Never, never have we had so many politicians and administrators with university degrees – and, by the way, do you notice the consequences?

A politician is a man who pushes you into the water, then expects your eternal gratitude for throwing you a lifebelt which immediately sinks.

Beg, borrow, or steal – governments do the first, then the second, finally the third.

If I paid my taxes as carelessly and dishonestly as the politicians spend them, I would have been in jail long since.

Politicians are generous souls, ever ready to help other people with money belonging to other people.

Politicians never made a poor country rich, but they are highly skilled at making a rich country poor.

I don't mind politicians being deceitful and mendacious. That is how it is with most of us poor humans. What I object to is the politicians' claim to be straightforward and truthful. That is the inexcusable deceit, the unforgiveable mendacity.

Don't be too angry at politicians for failing to honour their promises. If those promises really were honoured, we would be in an even worse financial mess than we are today.

If you try to buy one man's vote, using party funds, you are a criminal. If you try to buy a million men's votes, using public funds, you are a national political leader.

Some politicians can be bought, but most can only be rented.

Once you want something from another person, your corruption begins. That is why politicians are so morally corrupt; they want something from everybody – their vote. Can we argue from this that Eaton's and Simpsons and Dominion Stores are corrupt? They, too, want something from everybody – their money. But the big stores give refunds, your money back if not satisfied, which politicians sure as hell never do. Also, the big stores have to get your money off you every day; the politician wants your vote only once in four years, after that he doesn't give a damn about you.

There are high-class tarts and there are low-class tarts. A high-class tart selects her customers; a low-class one takes on any man, however brutal or sodden, providing he has the money. It seems to me that politicians come in the same category as the low-class tart; they will solicit and accept the vote of anybody who has one. Democratically elected politicians cannot confine their appeal to honest people, or to energetic people, or to intelligent people; they must also appeal to the dishonest, the lazy, the stupid – who in this society, as in any other, probably form the majority. As between getting ten votes from decent people, or fifteen votes from riff-raff, the politician will take the riff-raff; and that, as Dean Inge once remarked, is the consequence of a system which instead of weighing votes, merely counts them.

Most newspapers are very conscientious. They go to great pains to print accurate reports of the lies told by politicians, the pretexts advanced by bureaucrats, and the hallucinations entertained by economists.

An honest politician takes bribes from everybody who offers them, then votes according to his conscience.

A man who has failed in business can get elected to public office much more easily than one who has succeeded. Similarly, a rich man who has inherited his money can get elected to public office much more easily than one who has gone out and made it.

An iron law of history: the qualities needed to obtain power are the exact opposite of those needed to use it wisely.

History is simply a sequence of foolish men trying to clean up the messes left by foolish men who went before them and, in the process, leaving further messes to be cleaned up by the foolish men who come after them.

So you won the election. Great, your next problem is to get rid of all the people who helped you.

The politicians are in trouble enough already; telling the truth would only make it worse.

The politicians will do absolutely anything for the poor man, except take their hands out of his pocket.

If the poor and needy didn't have votes, the politicians would never give them so much as a passing thought.

Governments adore having emergency powers; that is why they create emergencies in the first place.

Schools are so great that kids must be forced to attend them, unions are so great that workers must be forced to join them, and politicians are so great that people must be forced to support them.

After finding out all the wonderful things governments can do, we are now finding out all the necessary things they can't do.

The politician tells you the beautiful things he is going to do when he is in power. He doesn't tell you the ugly things he will do to get that power – or the even uglier things he will do to hang on to it.

Following the disaster (military, political, economic), the men who obeyed the orders are punished; the men who gave them are promoted.

Governments don't make work; they only make paperwork, and you can't eat paper, you can't wear paper, you can't run your car with paper.

A committee charged with considering three possible courses of action soon has the choice narrowed down to eight.

A typical committee consists of five people. One does all the work, two go along with him, and the other two turn in a minority report.

When the politicians come up with a solution for your problem, you have got two problems.

To almost every problem, there is a solution – either so complicated that there is little chance of it being adopted, or so simple and logical that there is absolutely no chance of it being adopted.

By the time the experts bring in their report on the problem, it has become much worse. Or its nature has changed completely. Or it has solved itself and been replaced by three new problems, which mean more work for more experts.

After all is said and done, much has been said and practically nothing has been (or will be) done.

Governments find it easier to hire one hundred new civil servants than to fire an existing one.

I don't think anybody would deny that Canada has lots of space, I don't think anybody would deny that Canada is rich in all the materials used for building, and I don't think anybody would deny that Canada has a housing shortage. Isn't this a weird and wonderful situation? I'll hang it on the politicians and bureaucrats, who have so very, very much to do with housing. Those guys could produce a shortage of sand in the Sahara.

Canadians are weird; they look to Ottawa for the cure when Ottawa is, in fact, the disease.

The ghastly thing about postal strikes is that after they are over, the service returns to normal.

The bitterest men may be found in Ottawa. They are the ones who gave their loyalty to a cause, or a party, or a politician.

I don't see much hope for Canada until the voters are as cynical towards the politicians as the politicians are towards them.

Confederation is being killed off by a long and painful disease. The medical term for it is Ottawa.

North America won't recover its economic health until the mere mention of Washington or Ottawa makes people double up with laughter.

Don't complain about the weather; just be thankful Ottawa isn't running it.

When, and by whom, the first war was fought, I don't know. But I am sure that after it ended, the nations concerned got together and agreed they would *never* do such a naughty thing again.

Foreign aid – you lend another country money it will never pay back so it can buy things from you which it doesn't specially want, doesn't specially need, and doesn't know how to operate.

To expect gratitude among individuals is foolish enough; to expect it among nations is utter madness.

The nations should make an agreement that the next time one of them nabs a terrorist, he (she) shouldn't be shot, hanged, or even imprisoned. He (she) should simply be put ashore on an uninhabited island. Future terrorists who were caught would be put ashore on the same island. Then they could all have a great old time, terrorizing one another.

A nation is better off with bad laws which are strictly enforced than with good laws which are not. The one case tempers injustice with order, the other compounds injustice with anarchy.

A nation which doesn't have the guts to fight its own criminal class doesn't have the guts to fight the Russians or the Chinese. Russia and China know this and are acting accordingly.

In backward countries, the police execute the criminals; in progressive ones, the criminals execute the police.

A backward country is one where old ladies walk along the streets at night, and where parents don't warn their kids against talking to strangers.

A backward nation is one where the criminals stand in fear of the authorities. A progressive nation is one where the authorities and the general public which elects those authorities stand in fear of the criminals.

Poor countries don't have psychiatric treatment for criminals. They can't afford the psychiatrists. They can't afford the criminals, either.

In the ruling of nations, good men who are weak pave the way for bad men who are strong.

A reactionary is a man who thinks that doctors know more about medicine than politicians do, that builders know more about housing than bureaucrats do, that farmers know more about food than clergymen do, that bankers know more about money than university professors do, and that people who live in the North know more about Indians than people who live in Toronto do.

A liberal is a man who thinks that if you spend enough money on a donkey, he will turn into Secretariat.

A liberal is a person who is happy to give another person a helping hand – providing he can make a third person pay for it. He is even happier if he himself can make a profit out of the operation.

A liberal is a man who sees every side of the argument except his own.

A liberal is a man who hasn't been in New York in the last ten years; a conservative is a man who has.

The liberal knows how men ought to be governed; the conservative knows how men have to be governed.

A democrat is a man who loathes dictatorships but spends his holiday in one because he feels safer and gets better value for his money.

In a dictatorship, the people are afraid to tell the truth to the leaders. In a democracy, the leaders are afraid to tell the truth to the people.

To get anything done properly, you need a million dollars or a machine gun, and I am not at all sure about the million dollars.

The Western nations have many remarkable weapons, but the Chinese and Russians have three that can beat them all – order, discipline, patriotism.

It is not enough for the liberal democracies to have disorder at home; they are always trying to export it to other, less enlightened countries.

I wish North America would hassle its destructive people as efficiently as Russia hassles its creative ones.

A person who deliberately infected another with smallpox or cholera would be locked up, yet moving freely throughout our society are individuals who infect or try to infect others with fear, with anger, with guilt – diseases that destroy the soul as syphilis destroys the body.

If you believe the majority is always right, the gas ovens lie straight ahead.

Why do people believe that democracy, in itself, guarantees justice, decency, tolerance, human rights of any kind? Democracy is simply rule by the majority, and majorities have often been known to act abominably – for example, the

Protestant majority in Ulster, the African majority in Uganda, the white majority in many countries, including our own. Just as democracy has, in itself, no morality, neither do the political parties it produces. If it were clear, for example, that the majority of Canadians hated the Eskimos, each of our federal parties would come out with an anti-Eskimo program, and if, for example, the majority of Americans wanted the Indians exterminated, the Democrats and the Republicans would each argue that they could do the job more effectively. Justice, decency, and tolerance do not come from "the people," but from individual men and women who are just, decent, and tolerant.

The ultimate consequence of liberal democracy is that 15 percent of the people are in jail, 15 percent on pension, 15 percent on welfare, 15 percent on unemployment insurance, and 15 percent in the bureaucracy. The remaining 25 percent are working to support them.

Watching commercials on the tube, I realize something about Western civilization; even the dogs and cats are on welfare.

While the children of Japan and Germany were scrabbling around in the ruins, we were giving our children comfort and security and advantages. You can see the results in the trade figures – and that is only the beginning of it.

People who are picked up every time they fall down develop this peculiar habit of falling down.

When they talk about human rights, you know they are planning to take your money; when they talk about human needs, you know they are planning to take your home.

In the unplanned society, it's dog eat dog; in the planned society, both of them starve to death.

There is nobody quite so inferior as the man who insists that he is equal.

A strange and sad thing has happened in the English-speaking democracies. The minority, through violence and threats of violence, has become the majority. The majority, through timidity and apathy and nebulous ideas of "social justice," has become the minority.

The more governments do to help and protect people, the more people despise and defy them. Never in history have politicians handed out so many good things; never before have they been viewed and treated with such open contempt.

The man who loves everybody doesn't love anybody, and the man who wants to help all unfortunates everywhere will rarely be found helping one of them.

Everyone nowadays has rights – they are made up into codes and declarations – but hardly anybody has duties. Yet it seems to me that rights can only be exercised after duties have been fulfilled; in short, the duties come first. Thus, I as a human being have no God-given right to walk peacefully along Yonge Street; I must earn it by performing my own duty to keep the peace. As crime and disorder take over in our society, I think governments will have to pay somewhat more attention to this, but of course they won't. Can you really imagine Queen's Park setting up an Ontario Commission on Human Duties? Or Ottawa coming up with a declaration thereof?

If prison is such a terrible place, why do people do things which cause them to be sent there? And why do four out of five go back again?

Reading the papers, I notice all the excuses trotted out by, or on behalf of, criminals. He had no father. (Neither did I.) He grew up in poverty. (So did I.) He hadn't much schooling. (Neither did I.) Toronto is full of people who had far worse childhoods than I did – hunger, disease, war, concentration camps, torture. They have every excuse to rape, steal, and kill, but they don't. It seems to me we will never get the crime rate down until we stop thinking of people who rape and rob and murder as social problems and start thinking of them as rapists, robbers, and murderers.

It may well be that his criminality was caused by his "disadvantaged" upbringing; it may well be that in ten or twenty years, he will be "rehabilitated"; but it's now, right now, that you are looking down the muzzle of the gun he is pointing at you.

We are creating the kind of society where the criminal is out of jail before his victim is out of hospital.

There is nobody so sick as the people who think criminals are sick.

Our society is like an army which is so busy picking up the wounded and tracking down the deserters that it has neither the time nor the energy to fight any wars.

The great world sings love songs, preaches brotherhood, and campaigns for peace, all the while waging endless and ruthless war.

The world seems to me like a TV program in which the sound track bears absolutely no relationship to the picture.

If you obey its rules, the world will despise you. If you defy its rules, the world will break you. All the world asks about its rules is that you should give the appearance of obeying them, meanwhile snickering (as the world does itself) at their absurdity.

Money Talks

The lowest price you ever pay for anything is the one you pay with money.

You always get your money's worth out of every situation, especially when you know damn well that you didn't get it. That knowledge, that advance in experience, is itself worth the money.

Earning money is all very well, but I prefer simply making it.

You have to work twice for money; the first time to make it, the second time to keep it. The second is harder than the first.

There are doubtless things money won't buy, but one can't think of them at a moment's notice.

It is true riches don't bring happiness. Neither does poverty.

If you had saved your money instead of blowing it on tobacco, booze, cars, women, and horses, it would now be practically worthless.

When money is seen as a solution for every problem, money itself becomes the problem.

You used to go to the store with money in your purse and come back with food in your shopping bag. Now you go to the store with money in your shopping bag and come back with food in your purse.

Don't joke about wooden nickels; some day they might be worth more than paper dollars.

When money finally loses its value, will people stop holding up grocery stores? Of course not. They will point a gun, then run off with two tins of Spam and a box of cookies. As for the guys who rob banks, they will run off with the ashtrays, the ballpoint pens, and the red-headed foreign exchange teller.

There is one thing to be said for inflation. It enables you to live in a more expensive neighbourhood without moving out of your home.

There isn't the ghost of a chance to halt inflation until the politicians admit they caused it, and there isn't the ghost of a chance *that* will happen.

About inflation, every time the consumer price index goes up by 1 percent, the salaries of MPs should be reduced by 10 percent. That would straighten things out in a hurry.

If our politicians aren't doing very well against inflation, it is because they have only one hand to fight with; the other hand is busy turning the press.

Whenever anything (food, housing, medical care) is scarce or expensive, the politicians rush in with measures guaranteed to make it even more scarce, even more expensive.

One of the numerous causes of our inflation is the belief, almost universal among the Canadian middle class, that if you spend enough public money on him, the criminal will turn into a saint, the alcoholic into a teetotaller, the parasite into a productive member of society.

What Canadians seem to want is British order and American wages; they are more likely to end up with American order and British wages.

It is easier for the Americans to buy up Canada gradually than to conquer it suddenly. It looks better, too, and it makes the Canadians feel more comfortable.

The best friends of the poor people in Canada are the infinitely poorer people in Asia who make goods which the poor people in Canada can afford.

Canadian manufacturing will only bloom when our quality is as good as Switzerland's, when our prices are as low as Taiwan's, and when our products are snapped up by Brazilians, and that, as the saying goes, will be a frosty Friday.

I will believe the industrial nations are having an oil payments problem when they introduce the six-day week.

There is no nation so impoverished that it can't afford to buy up-to-date weapons for immediate or eventual use against its neighbours.

A country which doesn't have the guts to beat inflation doesn't have the guts to beat anything – or anybody – else.

In olden times, people believed in dragons, witches, and magic; today, they believe in progress, democracy, and economic planning.

A planned economy – ah yes, that is when the politicians make the plans, and the taxpayers make the economies.

Conferences on inflation are customarily attended by the politicians who caused it and the economists who showed them how.

I know plenty of wealthy drop-outs, but I have yet to meet a wealthy economist.

If our politicians are all that anxious to bring down food prices, let them quit their blathering and go to work on a farm. There are many vacant positions.

Since practically all of our economic problems were caused by politicians, I scarcely expect that they are going to be solved by politicians.

In the last depression, there was lots of food, no money, and no Help Wanted advertisements. In the next depression, there will be no food, lots of money, and the newspapers will consist mainly of Help Wanted advertisements.

Any Canadian who complains about the high cost of food should be sentenced to one month at hard labour on a farm.

I don't care if doctors get rich, or if bankers get rich, or if industrialists get rich; I just want the farmers to get rich, so they will keep the food coming.

The people who yell about the high price of food are the ones who never missed a meal in their lives. People who have really known hunger know that food is always worth whatever it costs. Similarly, people who have really starved never talk about starvation wages. To them, any wage looks good.

What is so great about eating beef? It is only a roundabout and expensive way of eating grass.

If milk cost a dollar a quart and if gin cost twenty dollars a quart, everybody would be screaming about the high price of milk.

I will believe the price of food is too high when I stop seeing those disgustingly obese people all over the place.

I will believe food prices are too high when the race tracks and beauty salons and cocktail bars close down for lack of business.

If the department stores had nothing to sell but rocks of various sizes and shapes and colours, the same crowds would be jamming the aisles, buying themselves into bankruptcy.

How carefully I write my name on a deposit slip! How sloppily I write it on a cheque!

So you pay cash? Your punishment will be to stand behind a little old lady who is using her credit card to buy a potted plant which she wants delivered to her sister in hospital at North Bay.

Credit cards are the modern, efficient way of buying. They

enable you to complete a transaction in fifteen minutes which, if you were using cash, would take all of five minutes.

If something people don't need costs $100 and is put on sale at $75, they will rush to buy it, figuring that with the $25 thus saved, they can buy something else they don't need.

The bigger and huskier the boy in the bus depot, the more likely he will ask if you can spare a quarter.

After living through all of them, I would say that the thirty years of post-war affluence did far more damage to the people of Canada than the ten years of pre-war depression.

When I was a kid, the poor people lived in slums which were privately owned and produced a whacking profit; today, they live in slums which are publicly owned and produce a whacking loss. This is progress?

Watching the human scene, I think of ten men sharing $100 among them. Each thinks he ought to get $15, and six of them probably will.

It doesn't matter how much money you have or don't have. You are poor if you think you are, and you are rich if you think you are. I always thought I was rich, even when I had to hoof it for lack of carfare.

A society which must coax children to eat is sick enough, so what are we to say of one which must coax dogs and cats to eat?

People complain that I am against the poor. Not so; I was born poor, brought up poor, remained poor for much of my life. What I am against is a political system which treats the poor as heroes, the rich as villains, and the middle class as suckers.

Anti-poverty programs do much to relieve poverty among the people who run anti-poverty programs.

What purports to be compassion for the poor is generally hatred and envy of the rich.

Many a rich man came up out of poverty, but I have never heard of one who came up out of welfare.

People who don't have to worry about money got there by worrying about money.

Poor people buy the junk that is being produced today; rich people buy the junk that was being produced a hundred years ago.

Everybody is happy when a rich man gets clobbered for cheating on his taxes. Especially happy are the middle-income people who are cheating on their own taxes.

We take for granted that a guy will go into law or banking or selling or engineering in order to make money. We will let him become a plumber or a truck driver in order to make money. But we are angry at the idea that anyone should go into medicine to make money, and we are furious if they actually do make it. We expect doctors and nurses (as once we expected teachers) to work for sheer dedication.

There are far more votes to be gained by promising to make the rich poor than by promising to make the poor rich.

You can't turn poor people into middle-class people by shoving tax money at them. All you will do is turn middle-class people into poor people.

If all of Canada's wealth were shared equally among all of Canada's people, there would be as much envy and anger and hatred as there is today. There would probably be more than there is today, because the people who managed on what they got would be cordially detested by those who couldn't.

When the hard times come, the rich will be living it up in their mansions, and the poor will be living it up in their subsidized housing. It is the dispossessed middle class who will be wearing the hand-me-downs and eating macaroni.

There is the guy who wants to help, and there is the guy who wants to be helped, and there is the guy who puts up the money for it. He is the one the other two laugh at.

In olden times, only the rich could afford to be degenerate; today it is open to everybody.

I would rather see power in the hands of the rich than in the hands of the mob. The rich have more sense than the mob; that is how they got to be rich.

I would sooner see Canada governed by millionaires than by clowns. The millionaires would at least have a vested interest in maintaining the value of the currency.

When someone talks about redistributing the wealth, I get very curious. He is giving away his house, of course, but to whom? Who gets the car? How will he share out his savings account? Who is going to get the snowmobile, the electric dishwasher, the colour TV? How do his wife and children feel about having the furniture taken from them and given to the needy? But I am polite, I was brought up not to ask personal questions, so I will never know the answers.

The Way We Are

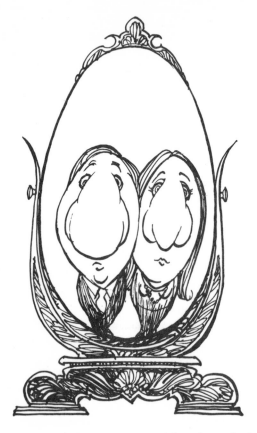

Human nature is funny – entranced by the splashing of a fountain, infuriated by the dripping of a tap.

Such is our nature that we would rather lose both gloves than one of them.

It sometimes happens with people, as with commodities, that the packaging is worth more than the contents.

What really takes will-power is to use someone else's bathroom without investigating the contents of the medicine cabinet.

Human beings can't be happy until they have got rid of their emotions – but at that point, I guess, they are no longer human beings.

Anglo-Saxon people are funny. They apologize for brushing against the man or woman they are sleeping with.

An age-old dilemma – if you let men do as they please, they (being human) will do terrible things. If you tell men what they are to do, you (being human) will tell them to do terrible things.

I don't practise discrimination. My life has been spent hiding out from people of every race, colour, and creed.

If you really want to make the world a better place, you could start by moving to the back of the bus.

The folly of the man who thinks he can make the world a better place is equalled only by the conceit of the man who thinks he can make it a worse one.

Oh, it's great these days. Everybody is counselling other people, or helping them, or educating them, or understanding them, or loving them, or relating to them, and, by the way, is anybody working?

People who talk about helping others might actually help others if they were not so busy talking about helping others.

People write me that they want to help others, and that is just great. But as I read on down the letter, it turns out that they themselves want help in order to help others – help from

Ottawa or Queen's Park or City Hall in the form of money, help from me in the form of money or free publicity. Ho hum, maybe someone should help me so that I can help them so that they can help others. Out of this one might get a hilariously funny situation – A helping B to help C to help D to help E and so on down to the object of all this philanthropic attention, Z, who – if I know human nature – will be lucky to get so much as a bag of peanuts.

If it is hard to change things, it is even harder to change people – to change one other person. All you can hope to do is to change yourself, make yourself a better person. A young man asked Thomas Carlyle how he could improve the world. Carlyle replied in his gruff Scottish way, "Make yourself an honest man; then you'll know there's one less rascal running around."

Kindly people are great, but if you want something done, you had better find some guy with a heart of stone.

When you are young, you want to love the whole world, and you want the whole world to love you. Later on, you discover how immensely difficult it is to get along with one other human being.

The young think the advantage of having money is that you can help other people. Later on, they find the advantage of having money is that you can protect yourself against other people. Money buys privacy and freedom; money buys beautiful distances between you and your friends and your enemies and your relatives and the rest of the human race.

If you really want to know about human nature, you could try opening a credit grocery next door to a cash liquor store.

Buying people with money may be dreadful, but what would they rather have? And what is a more effective way of keeping them in line? People can easily sever, or escape from, the bonds of love, friendship, and loyalty, but the bonds of money, they are something else again.

Breathes there the man with a soul so dead that he doesn't stick two fingers in the coin return box after completing a pay call?

Any man is willing to admit that the pop machine cheated him out of a quarter. Few are willing to admit that they shoved in another quarter and were cheated out of that one, too.

There is no way to buy a poor saint and no way to buy a millionaire, but there is a lot of promising territory in between.

The awful thing is not how much it costs to buy a man's soul, but how little.

You can buy the average fool for a couple of bucks, but a wise and honest man will cost you plenty. Being honest, he knows what he is worth, and being wise, he knows how to get somewhat more than he is worth.

People repay their debts not because they are honest, but so they can incur more and bigger ones.

When it comes to the money we owe other people, we are a bit on the vague side; when it comes to the money other people owe us, we have the memory of a computer.

Everybody is interested in a rich recluse, but nobody gives a damn about a poor one.

It's not that the rich have fewer troubles than the poor; it's just that theirs are more interesting.

The private life of a famous man is probably no worse than anybody else's; the difference is that people get to find out about it.

When the great man – call him Thaddeus Smith – kicks off, the newspapers tell you what marvellous things he did, how the country will cherish his memory for ever and a day, yea verily. Three months later, people are asking, "Thaddeus who?"

When the great man dies or steps down, the newspapers come out with reports, letters, and editorials, which make you wonder how the nation can manage without him. But somehow it manages to manage without him.

Great men usually start off as the solution. They end up as the problem.

Where we humans err is that we go from admiring a man's talent or accomplishment to admiring the man himself – and then we are disillusioned when he turns out to be something less than a hero, something less than a saint. Thus, a man is a great writer or painter or musician. Let's by all means admire his writing or his painting or his music. But let's not make the mistake of admiring the guy himself and then getting all upset when we learn that he beats his wife, or that he drinks too much, or that his cheques bounce. Few people are admirable in all ways, or indeed most ways; a great talent in one direction may indicate great failings in others.

We admire the cleverness of the scoundrel more than the innocence of the saint.

When a good man does a good deed, the world pays no attention. When a wicked man does a good deed, the world pays little attention. When a good man does a wicked deed, the world is delighted and scans the newspapers for every last detail.

It is the good people who gossip; the wicked people are too busy being wicked.

Live and let live – the two go together, and in proportion. The more fully and richly a man lives, the less he concerns himself with the lives of people around him; he lets them be. It is the people with small, dull lives who mess around with those of others. Fully alive people haven't the time for this, let alone the inclination.

Five little words which have prevented more sins and crimes than all of the priests and policemen put together – "What will the neighbours think?"

I don't mind what awful things people may say about me, as long as they have the decency to say them behind my back.

She didn't say a word all evening, just smiled and nodded her head as she listened to other people, and everybody remarked afterwards how witty and well-informed and intelligent she was.

Don't talk about yourself at a dinner party; that will be attended to after you have left.

It isn't the buildings, the climate, the environment, or the wealth that determines the quality of a city; it is the people who live there. If you were to exchange the population of Detroit with that of, let us say, Amsterdam, Detroit would become another Amsterdam, Amsterdam another Detroit.

Ask a man to define the public interest, and he will give you a pretty clear definition of his own.

If, like most of us, you have no set destination, it doesn't matter which direction you take; they are all fun; they will all teach you something.

Every man believes in fair play – fair to him, that is, and by his own definition of fairness.

Some people enjoy games which are played according to a fixed set of rules. Others prefer hockey.

What is wrong with people paying to watch a dog fight a dog, a cock fight a cock? They will pay plenty to watch a man fight a man.

Public opinion? Oh, that is what people think other people are thinking.

The private thoughts of practically anybody would shock practically everybody.

People don't ever change; they simply put on a different act.

Knowing what goes on behind my placid exterior, I have a strong suspicion of what goes on behind yours.

Many people know the tricks of the trade; few know the trade.

May you get what you want; it is the only way you will find out you don't want it.

Some people are like poinsettias; however real they may be, they still manage to look artificial.

None of us really knows what he or she looks like. We see ourselves only in a mirror and then with our own eyes, our own hopes, our own fears, our own vanity. Even when we see a photograph of ourselves, this remains the case; it's us looking at it and deciding it is a bad likeness, when, in fact, it is deadly accurate.

People who really want to lose weight don't talk about it; they just go ahead and do it. The ones who are always talking about it never shed a pound.

The kind of people who have the will-power to take off weight have the will-power not to put it on in the first place.

How desperately we search for someone who will understand us! How embarrassed we would be if we found someone who did!

One of the great human fallacies is to think we know or understand other people and can therefore predict what they will do. We never really know another person; we never really understand them; we never can tell what way they will jump. Thinking we can, we are often surprised by them, often disappointed; we feel that by some unexpected action they have been false to us and to themselves. But they were not being false to us or to themselves; they were being true to themselves and false only to the false image we had of them.

The moralist is depressed by the difference between the way men are and the way they ought to be; the humorist is delighted by the difference between the way men are and the way they pretend to be.

Optimists are always getting hideous disappointments; pessimists occasionally get beautiful surprises.

If we had an earthquake in one of our North American cities, the looters would do more damage than the quake, and the sightseers would cause more trouble than the looters.

People who don't have faith in human nature are forever cleaning up the mess made by people who do.

People who have given up on people get along pretty well with other people who have given up on people; you could form them into an organization – a non-encounter group, communicating by silences and absences.

So you have lost your faith in love, sex, marriage, religion, politics, and human nature? Great, now you are ready to enjoy life.

The cynic has a great life. If he doesn't get robbed on his way to work, it is a pleasant surprise that lasts with him all the rest of the day. If he does get robbed on his way to work, it proves he was absolutely right in his low view of human nature.

The alarm rings; you awake; you have returned to the scene of the crime.

It is my conviction that animals have lives just as complex and intellectual as mankind – that flies have tormented love affairs; that cockroaches argue whether there is a God; that worms pass along the important news of the day, that is, what is happening among worms.

Among animals, the higher species prey upon the lower. Among humans, it is the other way around.

Two cockroaches got into a conversation. One said, "Do you suppose there are higher forms of life than us cockroaches?" to which the other replied, "Don't be such a damn fool."

If one human being could spend one day without anger or malice or envy or disappointment, God would decide the whole experiment had been worthwhile.

Make the world a better place! Go through all of this day without hassling anybody, without criticizing anybody, without trying to put anybody down.

We seek advice from other people in the hope they will tell us to do what we have already decided to do. Then, if the decision proves wrong, we can blame them.

When the advice columnist gets a divorce, or when her children turn out badly, does that weaken her authority? Of course not, it strengthens her authority; she has joined the club!

We learn by making mistakes which hurt other people, but that is okay; they learn by making mistakes which hurt us.

'You can't lift yourself up by pulling other people down" – no, but pulling them down is satisfaction enough in itself.

When we correct someone on a point of fact, it is 10 percent to improve their knowledge, 10 percent to save them from committing the same blunder again, and 80 percent for the sheer joy of putting them down.

When a man says, "I'm going to be brutally honest with you," he means he is going to be brutal, but not necessarily honest.

We all manipulate other people and allow them to manipulate us. The thing is to do it with a good grace, to be amused by it, to recognize it as an inescapable part of the human condition.

People are alone because they want to be, or because they deserve to be, so you may as well leave them alone.

Spend twenty-four hours with a lonely person, and you will find out precisely why they are lonely.

Everybody you meet has a story to tell you – and just try to stop them from telling it.

Some people can stay longer in an hour than others can in a week.

People who have nothing to say, say it on the telephone.

People who have nothing to say, say it loudly and continuously and at the next table.

Every one of us can find the time to do what he really wants to do. The busiest man in Toronto, if he fell for some dame, would suddenly discover he had every evening free (or every afternoon, or every morning; there is no accounting for tastes).

I have noticed in life that people who have plenty of time to think about their troubles have plenty of troubles to think about.

Most of us talk about the injustices from which we suffer; few of us talk about the injustices we commit. For my own part, I figure that I am about as unfair to other people as they are to me, so I come out even.

People will forgive you anything, absolutely anything, if you make them laugh. An amusing man, like a beautiful woman, can quite literally get away with murder.

People ought to have the courage of their convictions. Unfortunately, those with convictions don't have much courage, and those with courage don't have many convictions.

Freedom and responsibility go together; unfortunately, for every one hundred people who want the one, there are at best five who want the other.

Strong people make as many and as ghastly mistakes as weak people. The difference is that strong people admit them, laugh at them, learn from them. That is how they became strong.

Few of us have the decency to practise what we preach, but most of us have the decency not to preach what we practise.

The bearded lady at the circus said, "Everybody's got something wrong with them. With me, you can tell what it is."

There are two kinds of people on this earth – those who keep their word and those who have a dozen excellent reasons why they were unable to keep their word.

It is not so much that people are liars; it's just that they are very, very weak. When someone says he is going to do this or that, he really means it; he actually hopes or wants to do it, but he will never get around to actually doing it, and he will have some excellent reason or excuse for his failure to do it. It is like taking off weight, I guess. The woman who is really determined to knock off ten pounds will do it; nothing can stop her. But such women are few. With the rest, it is a matter of hoping and wishing, so the fat stays on, and the companies engaged in the reducing business make their fortunes.

Broadly speaking, people are honest and won't steal anything that is red-hot or embedded in concrete.

As I grow older, I become more indulgent toward lies and hypocrisy. Most people need to lie; most people need to seem something other than (better than) they are. Demanding they be truthful and honest is like forcing them to stare at the sun.

Don't ask people why they said this or did that. They will probably lie to you. Worse yet, they might tell you the truth.

Lies, lies, lies, why do we go through life telling them? It is not so much, I think, that we are mendacious; it is that people get so upset when you tell them the truth.

There is the reason he officially announces. There is the reason he confides to his friends. There is the reason he divulges to his wife, and the reason he confesses to his mistress. There is the reason he tells himself. And finally, of course, there is the real reason.

People who get angry at you for telling them a lie are equally angry at you when you tell them the truth. They are the kind of people who enjoy being angry and who can always find a pretext for it.

Something I have noticed about people is the way they waste their anger on trivialities – a sullen store clerk, a rebellious coathanger, a timid driver in front of them. Using anger in these situations seems to me sheer waste – like doing the dishes in champagne. I am inclined to save up my wrath for occasions – and people – I deem worthy of it.

People get angry at you when they find out there is nothing to be gained by getting angry at you.

So someone has hurt and upset you? Don't just stand there, you fool; pass it along to someone else.

We don't mind being accused of something we didn't do; it makes us into heroes and martyrs. What we hate is being accused of something we did do.

You are best off being in the wrong. It may not be a beautiful place, but it is familiar, and you will never, never lack for company.

Relax, relax! People are not going to hate you for failing; they will hate you only for succeeding.

It is not my work to criticize other people; it is their work to criticize me – which they do, and I thank them for it, and this for some odd reason annoys them.

People tell me that I am prejudiced, unjust, intolerant, unfair, arbitrary. This is true; I know it; so why do they bother telling me?

Things are just right once you realize they are never going to be just right.

Three states in life – (1) you worry over criticism by other people; (2) you don't worry over it because you know they are wrong; (3) you don't worry over it because you know they are right. The third stage (when and if you reach it) is very restful.

You are getting there when you stop trying to please everybody. You have got there when you stop trying to please anybody.

There is only one way I can please other people, and that is by leaving them free to please themselves, and pleasing themselves is the only way they can please me.

Writers, composers, entertainers, and such know an awful truth – that it is easier to please a million people you don't know than to please one person you do know.

If you try to please yourself, you will at least please one person. If you try to please someone else, you will likely end up displeasing two.

Perhaps the greatest lesson a man must learn (and the learning of it may be painful) is to accept other people as they are from day to day and to accept situations as they arise moment by moment, meanwhile remaining true to himself – to himself alone.

You are a real man when the only things you want to do are the things you ought to do.

You are grown up when you don't need anybody. You may like or love particular people, but they are not essential to your life; they can and will be replaced when you so wish it – or, what is perhaps more likely, when they do.

A secure man is one who makes other people feel secure, and there are not many of them around.

What humanity needs is more joy – not more money or refrigerators or five-year plans, but more warmth and gaiety and delight in being alive, alive in a wonderful crazy world full of wonderful crazy people.

Between the Sexes

The things women do for love are almost as dreadful as the things men do for money.

The reason dogs' eyes are so sad is that they spend their lives being faithful to men.

At last it's possible to tell a young man from a young woman. He's the one wearing high heels.

I never thought I would live to see the day when the most important thing about a man was his hairdo.

Men don't remain babies all their lives; around forty, most of them become boys.

All men are bachelors, especially the ones who are married.

Men are creatures of habit. They hate to go home even when their wife is away in Europe.

There are many delightfully wicked men, but no delightfully good ones.

All interesting men are wicked, but it does not follow from this (as many foolish women seem to believe) that all wicked men are interesting.

A gentleman is one who, whatever has happened, acts as if nothing had happened.

A gentleman speaks loudly enough so that the person (persons) with him can hear what he is saying and softly enough so that nobody else can.

A gentleman is at a slight disadvantage in dealing with a lady and at a great one in dealing with a woman.

A gentleman doesn't waste his money on women; he wastes it on a particular woman.

One advantage of being a ladies' man is that you occasionally get to meet a lady.

A lesson few men ever learn is that the contents of a woman's heart and mind are more interesting than the contents of her pantyhose.

Men, do your duty! Somebody has to like women, and women don't.

When a man tells you how many affairs he has had, halve it; when he tells you how few, double it.

A man who mixes with women a lot might be described as a gourmet for punishment.

The man who looks up to women is a fool, but not so big a fool as the one who looks down on them.

A man is exposed to more temptations than a woman because he knows where to go looking for them.

All men make trouble for women; the difference is that strong men make a clean kind of trouble, weak men a dirty kind.

A man loves the woman who tries to help him out of trouble, but he hates the woman who tries to stop him from getting into it.

If men were a little more truthful, women would be a lot more miserable.

You should never allow a woman to think you are seeing her from a sense of duty. This is particularly the case when you are seeing her from a sense of duty.

Some men are so utterly base and treacherous that, having solemnly promised a woman they will stick to friendship with her, they stick to friendship with her.

Anton Chekov, the great Russian playwright, said, "Women, without the company of men, pine; men, without the company of women, grow stupid." I have no intention of growing stupid.

The wise man has many close women friends (that is how he became wise) but never introduces any of them to any of the others. He doesn't let any of them know that the others even exist.

It's quite simple, there is no mystery about it. The man who likes women and makes it clear to them that he likes them and makes it equally clear to them that he wants nothing from them other than the pleasure of their company will always have lots of women around – real smashers, too.

The man with women on his side will also have men on his side; the women will see to that. But the woman with men on her side need expect no help from women.

The fellow with manners will always have women around, but not quite so many as the fellow with manners and money.

Men who are interested in making money attract women who are interested in keeping them interested in making money.

Advice to a young man: have many different kinds of relationships with many different kinds of women, then take your wisdom (and your scars) into the stock market.

It's men who aspire toward sainthood. Women have more important things to do.

Men who are men never blame anybody but themselves, never criticize anybody but themselves, never try to improve anybody but themselves.

Men who are men have no time to yammer about their rights; they are too busy performing their duties.

Men who are men never complain about anything. If a situation bothers them, they act decisively – sometimes brutally – to correct or conclude it. But they never, never complain.

A man is the sum total of his responsibilities; as you diminish them, you diminish him.

Wherever you find one first-rate man, you will find others. First-rate men are attracted by competition and challenge; it is the second-rate men who look for security.

Advice to women: first-class men are difficult to acquire, easy to get rid of; with second-class men, it's just the opposite.

A girl becomes a woman in the school of men, and a boy becomes a man in the school of women. The difference is that women are eager to study, and men are not. Hence the surplus of women, and the shortage of men.

The trouble with women is men. The trouble with men is that the trouble with men is not women.

Women need men one hundred times more than men need women. That is the point a woman starts from, and that is the price she has to pay.

If you want to know the worst about men, talk to women. If you want to know the worst about women, talk to women.

Almost every woman has two faces – the one she shows to men and the one she shows to other women. Thus, a man might describe a woman as good-natured and generous; another woman might describe her as mean and vindictive. Both could be right.

Two women can get along if each has a man; two women can get along if neither has a man. But I don't think they can get along if one has a man and the other does not.

If a woman has a man coming in for dinner, she spends half

an hour tidying up her apartment; if she has another woman coming in for dinner, she spends a full day doing it.

If women were running the show, there wouldn't be any wars, but there would be some savage duels.

If women could hear politicians talking privately about them, they would never cast a ballot again.

She would rather that you brought her a daisy than that you sent her a dozen roses.

Send flowers to her at the office. It will please her. More important, it will infuriate all the other women.

I don't believe this business of a man "educating" a woman or of a woman "educating" a man. Every person has to educate himself or herself, but I will agree that the best place to do it is in the company of the opposite sex. I wouldn't say that I have learned anything *from* women, but I have learned almost everything *with* them.

It doesn't distress me when a woman is late for an appointment; all the women I know are eminently worth waiting for.

If you compliment a woman, she will say, "Do you really mean it?" If you insult her, she won't.

I once paid a woman what I thought was a very flattering compliment – "Being with you is almost as good as being alone" – but for some strange reason she didn't appreciate it.

A woman is beautiful if one man thinks she is, twice as beautiful if he tells her, three times as beautiful if he puts it in writing, four times as beautiful if he puts it into print, and now you know why (since God is female) I entertain mild hopes of going to Heaven.

When you tell a plain woman she is attractive, the glow on her face makes her so. Thus, what began as a lie ends as the truth.

The woman who has had many love affairs has in fact had only one – with herself, the various men concerned serving merely as props.

Vanity is stronger than modesty. A woman would rather have a man see her bottom than see her corn plaster.

"But what will people think about me?" My dear lady, your ego is showing. Other people are not thinking about you, and, if perchance you do enter their consciousness, they are wondering what you think about them.

When a woman who weighs 180 pounds manages to knock off 10 pounds, her first impulse is to rush downtown and stock up on clothes in size twelve.

"I can't understand it; I eat like a bird." Yes indeed, madam, like a vulture and twenty-five times a day.

To lose weight, you must be both a sadist and a masochist. The sadist sets the exercises; the masochist sets the table.

Take those scales out of the bathroom, madam; the right place for them is in front of your refrigerator.

It's very simple. You just pat her on the bottom, saying, "Please don't lose any more." She will fall into your arms, you poor devil.

You will know the depression has arrived when women stop buying new clothes.

A woman I know wears a tea cosy as a hat during the cold

weather. She says it's warm, it's comfortable, and everybody wants to know where she got it.

I will believe men and women are the same when I see equal numbers of them in the department stores.

The same woman who spends three hours choosing a pair of gloves expects the bill to be made up in five seconds.

In a big department store at any time you will find maybe five thousand women. Seven have come to buy something they need, eighty-four to buy something they don't need, and the rest to get in their way.

In the large downtown department stores, I encounter a few middle-aged women who seem to know where they are going and what they are doing. They are called salesladies.

The girl turns into a woman, the woman into a mistress, the mistress into a wife, the wife into a mother, the mother into one of those forlorn creatures you see drifting sadly and silently around the department stores.

Middle-aged women get the same punishment in Hell as they get on Earth – having to consort with other middle-aged women.

If women could have a healthy relationship with men, two-thirds of the women's clubs would go out of business.

Every woman enters middle age at fifty. Every other woman enters it at thirty-five.

Which would you rather look at – a blank sheet of paper, or one with interesting things written all over it? Exactly, and that is why I prefer the company of older women.

There is no such thing as an older woman – just women who have seen more of life and are therefore more interesting.

Talk to women under thirty about love; talk to women between thirty and forty about happiness; talk to women over forty about money and how it brings happiness and love.

Zeus understood women; he descended upon Danae in a shower of gold.

It's men who think money should be taken from the rich and given to the poor. Women are more sensible; they think it should be given to them.

Spend it on women. You may not get your money's worth out of it, but they will.

Women don't really want possessions. They want love. If they don't get love, they will take possessions as the next best thing – diamonds and mink coats and all the rest. But these things don't make a woman happy; only love can do that. The woman who "has everything" has nothing, and she knows it, and the world knows it, too. It is the woman who is loved that has everything.

Women like a man who says very little. They think he is listening.

A woman finds it easier to forgive the man who broke her heart than the one who ignored her.

In the course of an ordinary day, I talk to one woman who is miserable because there is no man in her life and another who is happy because she just got rid of the man in her life.

Two ways to get in trouble with a woman: (1) being foolish

and attempting to understand her, and (2) being wise and making no effort to understand her.

A woman is happy when pursuing a man who appears unattainable and furious when she finds out he really is.

A woman likes a man who doesn't hassle her. It conserves her energy so she can hassle him.

The woman who wants to quarrel with a man will always find a good reason for it. If he is a gentleman, he will, of course, provide her with several good reasons, so she can choose the one that suits her best.

Two men irritate a woman – the one who wants to be with her all the time, and the one who doesn't.

A well-bred woman never quarrels with anybody except her husband.

It is typical of a woman's generosity that she forgives her lover for the harm he is doing to her husband.

It is much easier for a woman to corrupt a saint than to reform a sinner. Much more fun, too.

Society is much more tolerant toward the single woman who adopts a kid than toward the single woman who gives birth to one. The woman who produces her own likely got some fun out of it.

Most of the single women want to get a husband, most of the married women want to get rid of one, so why don't they just make a deal?

Women grow tired of associating with other women, so they

get married and spend the rest of their lives associating with other women.

Those TV commercials leave me puzzled. When women who are attractive, intelligent, and presumably educated get together, do they really discuss the best way to clean the toilet bowl?

We would be in the deepest trouble if housewives were as stupid as the radio and TV commercials make them out to be.

I mix a lot with housewives (my favourite people) and over-hear many conversations among them. I must confess I never hear them talking about detergents or floor wax or toothpaste; I never hear them gurgling to each other about canned soups or packaged cereals. The housewives I encounter talk about men and kids and schools and books and sex and marriage and politics and movies and travel, but then I am an odd sort of person, and I possibly attract an odd sort of housewife.

It's easy to entertain a housewife. She will enjoy any meal, even the simplest, that has been cooked by somebody else.

The way to a woman's heart is through the door of a good res-taurant.

Some women are buried in coffins, but the majority are bur-ied in bungalows.

Every woman would like to go on a trip – but not with her husband, and not with her children, and not with another woman, and not alone.

To every man she meets for the first time, a woman says, in effect, "Are you the one?" She generally gets the answer in five minutes. He isn't.

The worst loneliness is that of married women. Single women are lonely, but there is always the chance they will meet an interesting man, and they are free to make use of that chance. The married woman isn't; the price she pays for love, or even friendship, with a man other than her husband can be the loss of her children, her home, everything. She is alone behind bars, the days crawl by, and every one of them makes her a little bit older.

A widow weeps with one eye and looks around with the other.

My mother, a widow, had a dog to which she was very attached. Then a man came into her life, and she focussed her attention on him. After that calamity, she went back to the dog.

She married a man for companionship and didn't get it, so she had children for companionship and didn't get it, so she had an affair for companionship and didn't get it, and now she has goldfish.

Marriage

A successful marriage, if such there might be, would take its cue not from romantic poems or love songs but from the British North America Act – "Peace, order and good government."

Every woman has a natural instinct to turn a good lover into a bad husband.

Falling in love is great, but it's a poor reason to get married.

I'd place more faith in a love that resulted from marriage than in a marriage that resulted from love.

A woman should not marry for love; that's crazy. She should marry the guy because she likes him (which is quite different from loving him), or because he is rich, or because he is obviously going to be. After marrying him, she might possibly get to love him – as Moliere says, love is often the fruit of marriage – and if she doesn't, well, there is no great harm done.

When it comes to love, women want to fly first-class; when it comes to marriage, they will settle for a seat on the bus.

Bernard Shaw said that marriage combines the maximum of temptation with the maximum of opportunity. He was, as usual, half right.

I am scandalized by men and women who live together without a marriage licence. I am equally scandalized, of course, by men and women who live together with one.

What is so wrong with a marriage of convenience? It has at least the advantage of being convenient.

Belong to someone? No, never! But belonging *with* someone, that is something else again.

Marriage does not guarantee you are going to be happy; it simply guarantees you are going to be married, and, in our day and age, it doesn't always guarantee that.

Marriage does not guarantee that you will always have someone to love or even to like; what it does guarantee is that you will always have someone to blame.

Marriage is a fifty-fifty relationship which according to each of the partners is ninety-ten.

Marriage is a romance in which the hero dies in the first chapter and the heroine in the second.

A happy marriage. She served him rice pudding once a week and he hated it but told her it was delicious, so she kept on serving it (PS She hated it, too). He took her to the symphony once a week, and she hated it but told him it was marvellous, so he kept on taking her (PS He hated it, too).

There is more theatrical talent around than you might think. Any marriage that holds together produces a skilled actor, a talented actress. They know their roles and play them well.

Just about any man and woman can share a bedroom, but sharing a bathroom – ah, that is something else again.

Before the wedding, you discover 10 percent about him; after the wedding, you get the remaining 90 percent thrown at you.

You don't marry one person, you marry three of them – the person you think they are, the person they are, and the person they are going to become as the result of being married to you.

It doesn't matter much whom you marry, since you find out inside of a week it was somebody else.

Happily married couples never tell each other the truth about anything; that is why they are happily married.

A couple who don't need each other might manage pretty well, so long as neither one of them admits it.

The motel clerk is always pleased when they ask for a room

with twin beds – "Oh, goodie; nice, quiet, respectable, married people."

I notice at parties that the woman who proclaims she is happily married is the one who is drinking the most.

You can always tell married people at a party; they are the ones who don't want to go home.

You never know the truth about anyone else's marriage; you only know the truth about your own, and you know exactly half of that.

There is one marriage even stranger than your own – that of the people next door to you.

And yet when all, all, all is said about the horrors of marriage, we still must admit that single people don't seem any happier.

Every woman should be married and no man. That is the way Disraeli put it, and that, as I look around, seems to be the way it is.

Behind every successful man there stands an astonished mother-in-law.

Nearly all men are married. Some are married to cars, some to booze, some to money, some to power, some to fame, some to golf, some to gambling. A small minority are married to a woman.

Husbands, like politicians, soon forget their campaign promises.

Tell a guy his wife is an idiot, and he will probably agree with you; suggest she is anything less beautiful than Helen of Troy, and he will probably slug you.

In the beginning, you want a woman who is Raquel Welch and Sophia Loren and Glenda Jackson all put together. In the end, you settle for one who will let you read the newspaper in peace.

The reason a woman holds a man's arm walking down the street is that it looks better than having him on a leash.

A double-ring ceremony – one on each finger, one through each nose.

If he won't take orders from you, he won't take orders from any other woman, and isn't that the way you would rather have it?

Husbands should never teach their wives to drive. It is liable to bust up the car, or the marriage, or both.

There is the man who turned to drink because she didn't marry him, and there is the man who turned to drink because she did.

A radical is a single man. A liberal is a married man. A moderate is a married man with one child. A conservative is a married man with two children. A reactionary is a married man with three children.

By the time a man is mature enough to make a good husband, he is more likely to make a good corpse.

A man annoys a woman by his absence, or his presence, or by his absence during his presence.

We despise the poor man who marries a rich woman; he is a fortune hunter. But the poor woman who marries a rich man, why she is just smart.

A woman can't win. If the guy dislikes his work, he will never be happy, and if he likes it, he will never be home.

A woman told me about her husband, "All he cares about is making money, and he is so pooped out from it that he goes to bed every night at ten." I thought to myself, "What are you complaining about? Compared to most of the married women I know, you have got it made."

"My wife doesn't understand me" – my dear fellow, if she understood you, she would have left you a long time ago.

A husband suspects one other man; a wife, all other women.

Many a man would more easily forgive his wife for being unfaithful than for putting a dent in the new car.

When a man discovers his wife is having an affair, he is not so much angry as stunned. How could anybody take the slightest interest in her?

The world regards war with the same horror, the same repulsion, as suburban couples regard adultery.

We all have our flings and should. But in the end, we go back to the people with whom we are comfortable, the ones who accept us for what we are, the ones with whom we have natural and easy communication.

The man who doesn't realize how little it takes to make a woman happy will end up complaining how much it takes to make a woman happy.

Every man needs an understanding wife, who will occasionally turn out to be someone else's.

A woman would far sooner that her husband spent every

night drinking with a bunch of stupid men than that he occasionally had lunch with an intelligent woman.

A wife need not fear the woman her husband likes, or even loves. He will probably be back. The woman she has reason to fear is the one he pities.

A woman told me she worked her head off to put her husband through medical school. He graduated and is now doing so well he can afford a mistress.

The vast majority of men are polygamous; so are the vast majority of women. The difference is that men are polygamous in reality, women in their imagination. Perhaps the women get the better part of the deal.

If fidelity is all that important to you, don't marry a man, marry a dachshund.

Half of the married women fear their husband will leave them, and the other half wish he would.

A woman getting married trades her freedom for his love, shortly to discover she hasn't either.

Before marriage, he promised her everything but the kitchen sink; after marriage, the kitchen sink was all she got.

She started off wanting to touch the hem of his garment; she wound up having to launder the damn thing.

If you hadn't thought how wonderful he was when you married him, you would not be thinking how horrible he is today.

After she got engaged, she thought, "What have I done to deserve this?" After she got married, she thought, "What have I done to deserve this?"

Some day, your prince will come! He will come ten years after you gave up waiting for him and married a creep.

Almost every woman I know has, as I put it, traded down in her love or marriage. Her man is okay, perhaps, but he is not really equal to her. I could count on the fingers of one hand the women I know who in love or marriage have a man they can look up to.

Every woman wants to be married to a celebrity, except the ones who are.

In their hearts, all women believe it is the business of men to make money and their own to spend it; if possible, while their husbands are alive; if not, then afterward.

Women do not resent the widow who has inherited her husband's money; they do resent the spinster who has inherited it from an uncle or grandfather or such. The widow, they feel, has earned it. She served her term.

Practically every woman is looking for a man who will be as happy to see her at 10:00 A.M. as at 10:00 P.M.

B. told me, "A husband is always there when you don't want him, and a lover is never there when you do."

Mixed marriages? The problem is not that he is Jewish and she is Gentile or that he is Italian and she is Japanese, the problem is that he is a man and she is a woman; that is the mix of it.

Some people have worked out the formula for a perfect marriage; others are married.

Most of us are pretty tolerant. We will accept the faults and follies and failings of everyone except the person we are married to.

Every time a woman gives a man a piece of her mind, she loses a piece of his heart.

The world is full of battling couples who would probably get along pretty well with each other if they weren't married.

If you keep on giving your husband a piece of your mind, you will end up with no mind left. No husband either.

Some couples get along in a manner of speaking and some in a manner of not.

The loudest noise in this world is that of a couple who are not speaking to one another.

Four things that might, just might, help to make a successful marriage – silences, secrets, solitudes, separations.

Young people nowadays are very impatient. They want to fight with each other immediately, instead of waiting until they are married.

For the first five years after marriage, he wants the same working hours as she has; after that, he will settle for different ones.

In the beginning, she was married to him and he to her; now each of them is married to a house.

If couples loved each other somewhat less and liked each other somewhat more, they might get along somewhat better.

The man or woman you love stays in your life for a while; the man or woman you like stays in your life a bit longer; the man or woman who is useful to you stays in your life for years and years. A man or woman can of course play two of these roles – being liked and being loved, or being liked and being useful, or being loved and being useful. With very great luck, he or she might play all three.

Detente? Ah yes, that is what you get – or may reasonably hope to get – after you have been married thirty years.

At the age of forty or thereabouts, everybody should be allowed to do one thing he or she has always wanted to do. For example, he might go and shoot lions in Africa; she might spend a week shopping in New York; he might buy a case of Scotch and hole up for a week at the Mark Hopkins in San Francisco; she might fly to Hawaii and come back with a grin on her face. If doing this one thing would finish your marriage, your marriage deserves to be finished. In fact, I think if husbands and wives did occasionally bust out and do one adventurous thing, make one dream at least come true, an awful lot of marriages would last an awful lot longer.

Younger couples are held together in shared happiness and hope, older couples in shared sorrow and disappointment.

One of the many difficulties with modern marriage is that husbands and wives – save those with several small children – are no longer tired when they come to the end of the day. In olden times, the evening found them worn out from grinding toil, wanting only to sleep. Now machines are doing most of the work; husbands and wives come into the evening full of physical and emotional energy. That is good for making love, perhaps, but it is equally good for making trouble.

The best way for a man and a woman to live together is to live separately.

For the first five years of marriage, a double bed. For the next ten years, twin beds. For the next ten years, separate rooms. For the rest, separate homes.

Most of the couples in Toronto are separated, but they are still living together.

Kids can't wait to get on the train and, once on, can't wait to get off it. Let's see now, was someone saying something about love and marriage?

When a love affair falls on evil days, pride moves in and takes over. He wants to be the one who breaks it off; she wants to be the one who breaks it off; the question is who will get there first.

Some people get divorces for trivial reasons such as infidelity and some get divorces for extremely serious reasons, such as impoliteness.

A divorce lawyer told me, "The important thing in marriage isn't love; it is respect. When that goes, everything goes."

A woman told me that her husband has not spoken to her for five years. But she is still living with him, of course – for the sake of appearances, for the sake of the children. In short, like many other married women, she has chosen death as her way of life, and all we have to do now is bury her.

A woman I know opposes love because it leads to marriage, opposes marriage because it leads to divorce, and opposes divorce because it leads to remarriage.

Family Life

Getting married is the way you find out whether you should be married or not. Having children is the way you find out whether you should have children or not.

The man who owns his home had better own a hardware store while he is at it.

When a man marries and has children and buys a house, he has committed practically all of his life and his lifetime earnings to other people. At the time, he hotly defends the decision; later on, he will wonder about it; he may even regret it. But he will rarely admit that regret. It is his cross; he chose it; he will bear it bravely. And in any case, what else could he or should he have done? There is something in most of us humans that fears freedom; it is easier to get ourselves deeply and irrevocably committed; it is easier to be a slave.

The first twenty years of your life are ruined by your parents; the next twenty years are ruined by your children; doctors, lawyers, and tax collectors look after the rest.

There will be peace in the world when there is peace in the family. Yes, indeed, you may call me a bleak pessimist.

A woman who went to Florida with her husband and children told me afterwards, "It wasn't a change of scenery, just a change of sink."

There are four classes of travel – first, second, third, and with children.

One of the punishments in Hell is to drive ten thousand miles with three small kids and a dog in the back seat.

There is one argument for expensive restaurants; people don't take their small children there.

Families fight, not because they are families, but because they are human beings living together under one roof. I think if you took five unrelated people of differing ages and sexes and made them live together under one roof, you would have about the same amount of nastiness and injustice and guerrilla warfare as you have in the ordinary home.

Every family needs a black sheep. He or she makes the other members seem a little bit better than they really are.

A woman I know operates on the principle that her husband comes first, she herself comes next, and the children come third. Her husband says no, she should operate on the principle that she herself comes first, he comes next, and the children third. They agree, at least, that the children come third, and that is a refreshing change from the average North American household, which the children dominate and often tyrannize.

There is the household where the parents hassle the kids; there is the household where the kids hassle the parents; there is the household where the parents and the kids hassle each other, and there must be some other kind of household, but I never get to hear about it.

A marriage centred on the children will destroy the children – also the husband, also the wife, also the marriage.

I used to wonder about the people who adopt children; now I am starting to wonder about the people who produce their own.

Nature requires you to love your kids, but it doesn't require you to like them. The same mother who would fight like a wildcat to protect her son's life can't stand having him around the house.

When a mother is away, she thinks all the time about children who aren't giving the slightest thought to her.

Every boy needs three fathers – a father in the home, a Father in Heaven, and Father Patrick O'Donovan, who comes around each week with the catechism and a big stick.

A woman may not love her kids, she may not even like them, but by golly, they are her kids, and she will walk through fire for them.

Family life seems to me an uneasy compromise between the love the parents feel for the child and the resentment the child feels toward the parents.

I would guess that for every marriage being held together by the children, there is at least one being torn apart by them.

If the kid announces he hates his parents, that is okay; it's normal; he is normal. But if the parents even suggest they dislike the kid, they are considered heartless monsters.

You should treat your children as strangers whom you happen to like – if, that is, you happen to like them.

If you treat your children with respect and set them a good example and give them firm but kindly guidance, you may be reasonably sure that they, like everybody else's children, will turn out disastrously.

If your kids turn out well, you have a good topic for conversation; if they turn out badly, you have an even better one.

No matter how you bring up your children, you turn out badly.

There is this to be said for the calamity of being a child: it toughens you up for the calamity of being a parent.

Three good ways to get revenge on your children – (1) die, leaving nothing but debts; (2) become a burden to them in your old age; (3) commit (around sixty) some picturesque crime which will bring shame on their heads and support you more or less comfortably in prison for the rest of your life.

You spend an awful lot of money on your kids, and in the end there is not much to show for it. But if you had spent all that money on yourself, what would there be to show for it?

A lot of parents say they are pleased with the way their kids turned out, and some of them actually mean it.

It's best for a child to have two parents; that way, each can blame the other for the way he turns out.

Some parents bear their children like a garland, others, like a cross.

If the good Lord were at all considerate, He would arrange things so that when the children He sends turn out to be unsatisfactory, they could be returned.

I asked a man of about fifty if his children had turned out as he expected. He answered, "Yes – unfortunately."

After the bird has flown the nest, does it come back for dinner every Sunday, bringing its own young?

When your daughter gets married, you aren't shedding a responsibility, you are adding a new one, and other new ones will come along in due time.

Correct this sentence: "I will be glad when the children are up and away, and I don't have to worry about them any more."

Isn't it true in most cases that the parents need the children a whole lot more than the children need the parents?

People who "live for their children" are doing something, but it isn't living – and the amount of gratitude they will get for it wouldn't cover a dime.

Don't be too hard on your children because they are ungrateful. They will be punished enough when they look for gratitude from their own children.

People who don't have children are lonely in their old age – as lonely, you might say, as people who do.

A childless couple usually have one without being aware of it. Sometimes it is the wife, more often the husband.

I always wanted my kids to have such full, free, and interesting lives that they would never have time to give me the slightest thought.

I am beginning to see the predicament of modern youth. It is much easier to fight your way out of poverty and neglect than to fight your way out of comfort and solicitude.

Part of the generation gap concerns poverty. To me, it means not having food; to the young, it means not having colour TV.

Of course children should battle their parents; how else will they learn to battle the world?

When I was a kid, you didn't dare say there was nothing to do, because your parents would rapidly find something.

Everybody was delighted by the arrival of the little stranger. Some sixteen years later, they were wishing they could get rid of the big stranger.

When a man drowns, his whole past life is supposed to flash before him. It is my theory that when a child is born, his future life flashes before him. That is why he lets out such a holler.

An effective method of birth control would be to have the father look after the kid for the first month.

If your child resembles you in any way whatsoever, you know that a terrible mistake was made at the hospital.

Certainly your child is different from you. Nature doesn't make the same mistake twice.

When I was a kid, creepy adults used to tell me, "These are the best years of your life." I thought to myself, "If these are the best, what are the worst going to be like?"

When your parents say, "We won't talk about it any more; let's just forget it and pretend it never happened," what they mean is that in a week or so, they will once more be rubbing your nose in it.

The reason grandparents and grandchildren get along so well is that they both have the same enemy.

An embittered woman of perhaps fifty told me, "The only good thing I got out of my children was grandchildren."

The young have everything you longed for when you were young – and they are just as miserable.

We are none of us infallible, not even the youngest of us.

The young are funniest when they pretend to be shocked by the world's pretenses.

Everybody likes babies, most people like children, and there must be somebody around who likes teenagers.

Kids need love when they are small, unable to fend for themselves, and nature generally sees that they get it. But as they grow older and wiser and stronger, they have less need of love – parental love, at any rate. That is why I feel it is quite okay for parents merely to tolerate their teen-agers or even to dislike them. They did the loving when the loving was required; now it's over.

Glumly viewing her teen-age son, a woman told me, "I

wanted a girl, my husband wanted a boy, the Lord must have tried to please both of us."

Heredity is what causes the parents of teen-age children to look sideways at one another.

A mother suggested to me that when kids reach sixteen (or seventeen or eighteen) they should sign a contract with their parents agreeing that neither party owes the other anything except common (or uncommon) courtesy.

So your parents don't understand you? Be thankful for that; if they did, they would throw you out of the house.

I hate to tell you this, young man, but your parents find you just as boring as you find them.

When I was young, you expressed your dislike of your parents by leaving home; today, you express it by staying.

As children grow up, they must learn to depend less on their parents. What is equally important is that their parents should learn to depend less on them. The parents of teenagers should be developing new lives, new friends, new interests that have nothing to do with their children. Thus, the kids are free to do what they must – grow and go.

If God gave you good parents, you should thank Him for it; if He gave you bad parents, you should thank Him for giving you the excuse to walk out on them.

To the teen-agers, I am inclined to say, "Your marriage will be as successful as that of your parents." They look at me aghast. To the parents, I am inclined to say, "Your children's marriages will turn out as well as yours." They, too, look at me aghast.

If (as sometimes happens) a guy is eighteen and married and

still going to high school, who writes the note to explain why he is late or absent? His wife? His mother?

How easy it is to respect, even love, your parents when you no longer have to live with them.

We are protective toward our young people and won't allow them to attend movies in which the characters use language of the kind used by young people.

There are certain short vulgar words which relate to the bedroom and bathroom. If I used these words in a university or a high school or even a junior high school, I don't think anybody would be shocked. That is the way they talk themselves. But if I used words like honour, duty, loyalty, the students would be at worst horrified, at best embarrassed.

The purpose of the school is to take in small, ignorant savages and turn out large, ignorant savages.

If children were taught to speak, they never would.

One sure way to prevent your kids from reading dirty books would be to buy such books specially for them.

The kids count the days until school lets out; the mothers count the days until school lets back in.

School goes back the first week in September, not because the weather is bad (it isn't), not because the crops are in (they aren't), but because the parents can no longer stand having their kids around.

Some students drink from the fountain of knowledge, but most simply gargle with it.

The students don't want to learn the subject. What they want to learn and in most cases do learn, is how to obtain a document *saying* they have learned the subject.

When kids do work that is artificial and unproductive, it is "education." When they do work that is real and productive, it is "child labour."

Sitting in a classroom is an excellent preparation for life – assuming your life is to be spent sitting in a classroom.

The high school graduate who has taken French enjoys the advantage of being illiterate in two languages.

If he is smart enough to go to university, he is smart enough to go to work instead. One year in an office, factory, or mine will teach him more than three years in any classroom.

Our students used to put themselves through college by waiting on table. Now the taxpayer has to put them through college; he's the one who is waiting on table.

In the old days, a boy went to work to support his mother. Now she goes to work to support him – to keep him in high school and put him through university, and you know how much thanks she will ever get for it.

Parents are much more proud of a son who is an unsuccessful lawyer than of one who is a highly paid chef.

In olden times, the carpenter's son got employment as a carpenter; today (and to the pride of his father) he is an unemployed Ph.D.

The first generation dug ditches; the second ran a corner store; the third operates a chain of supermarkets; the fourth has its Ph.D., is under psychiatric attention, and may eventually be able to do some light, simple form of work.

If the Pied Piper of Hamelin came to Ontario and took away all the children, our education costs would triple.

Growing Older

Be careful how you spend the first thirty-five years of your life; after that, they are your face.

When you are old, the purpose of life becomes magnificently simple and obvious. It is to keep on living.

When you are young, you love holidays because they are a break in the routine. When you are old, you hate holidays for precisely the same reason.

When you are young, you swap stamps; when you are middle-aged, wives; when you are old, symptoms.

When you are young, you are shocked by the hypocrisy of others; when you are old, you are amused by your own.

When you are young, the most important word is "in"; later on, the most important word is "out."

When you are young, you want to grab everything in sight; when you are middle-aged, you want to keep the things you have; when you are old, you let them go, let them drift away, let someone else worry about them.

You don't need much money when you are young, and you don't need much money when you are old, but in between you need enough to sink a battleship.

When you are twenty, you watch the feast through a window. When you are thirty, you get to eat some of the leftovers. When you are forty, you are invited to dine. When you are fifty, you find you have been stuck with the tab. When you are sixty, you plead ill health and go for a walk instead.

When you are young, you want people to love you; when you are middle-aged, you want them to like you; when you are old, you wish to God they would leave you alone.

When you grow old, you don't want to make new friends; the ones you have already are trouble enough.

Which, I wonder, are the more pathetic – the old who are putting in time until they die, or the young who are putting in time until they live?

When you are young, you stay alive out of hope; when you are middle-aged, out of habit; when you are old, out of spite.

When you are young, you ask, "Why should he have a nicer mother than I have?" Later, you will ask, "Why should he have a prettier wife than I have?" Still later, you will ask, "Why should his children have turned out better than mine did?"

When you are young, you hesitate to make advances for fear they may be rejected; later on, you hesitate to make advances for fear they may be welcomed.

When you are young, you tell painful truths; when you are middle-aged, you tell pleasant lies; when you are old, you just remain silent.

When you are young, you see both the problem and the solution. When you are middle-aged, you don't see that there is any solution. When you are old, you don't see that there is any problem.

When I was young, I had five ambitions – to read all the books in the world, to eat all the food in the world, to drink all the booze in the world, to see all the countries in the world, and to go out with all the women in the world. And how did I manage? Well, I have an awful lot of reading still ahead of me.

It is great when you are young and love everybody; it is great when you are old and hate everybody; the bad years are the ones in between.

It is sheer folly for the old to advise, or try to advise, the young. No way, man; the young will have to go the full course; they must learn every bit of it for themselves, out of their own experience. What, then, is the function of the old with respect to the young? They should do what I do – sit back, watch, cackle, enjoy.

For the first half of your life, people tell you what you should do; for the second half, they tell you what you should have done.

At twenty, you are horrified by the thought that people of thirty have sex; at thirty, you are horrified by the thought that people of forty do; at forty, you are horrified by the thought that people of fifty do; at fifty, you are horrified by the thought that people of sixty do; and, at sixty, you are just plain horrified.

God is merciful. No woman knows which time is the last that she will ever be kissed, and no man knows which time is the last that a woman will ever look speculatively at him.

Nobody wants you when you are old. True enough, but I am not sure people want you that much when you are young. I'd say that if you want to be desired, you had better make yourself desirable; if you want to be needed, you had better make yourself necessary; if you want to be loved, you had better make yourself lovable. Nobody in this world has a right to be wanted or needed or loved; nobody in this world has a right to anything.

Derrick Murdoch of Toronto told me, "You're still young if you can feel guilty."

You are getting old when you prefer the polite hypocrisy of adults to the vulgar sincerity of the young.

A man of sixty talking to a woman of twenty is allowed to describe himself as being old. But he had better not try it if he is talking to a woman of fifty.

The reason they give you a Westminster chime clock when you retire is so you will sit there like a dummy, watching the hands crawl slow – ww – ly arou – oun – dd.

I am told many women of sixty and over are entering the labour force. Their husband has retired, they can't stand having the old man around the house all the time, so they go out to work themselves.

Almost everybody wants to have a long life, but hardly anybody wants to be old.

A bad memory is useful in one respect; it enables you to recall the good old days.

At my age, one remembers many interesting things, some of which actually happened.

Happy the man who loses his interest in sex before he loses his capacity for it.

As you grow old, you lose your interest in sex, your friends drift away, your children ignore you. There are many other advantages, of course, but these would seem to me the outstanding ones.

Any man who is proud of his past has lived a very different life from the rest of us.

As we grow old, other people drift away from us, and we in turn drift away from other people. Thus, Nature prepares us to do alone what must be done alone.

A man who has run out of steam can have marvellous relationships with women – but only with women who themselves have run out of steam.

By the time a man is wise enough to handle a love affair properly, he has lost much of his interest and most of his capacity.

It is always disgusting to watch people pursuing the vices

which no longer appeal to you, or of which you are no longer capable.

I am at the age where I think I would like to see so-and-so, but it is too much trouble to write (she might be away somewhere) and I hate using the telephone. (Even if I did ring her, the line might be busy or there might be no answer.) So I wander over to Yonge Street thinking I might (but knowing I won't) bump into her.

I am so old, I can remember when young people tried to make themselves look attractive.

I am so old, I can remember when kids went to the movies – and when there were movies they could go to.

I have reached the time of life when I don't care where I sit on the plane.

Certainly we change as we grow older; whole parts of us are buried in the pasts of other people; whole parts of them are buried in our own.

My mother told me, "You have to eat a peck of dirt in a lifetime." Yes, and you have to go through a peck of people in a lifetime – friends, lovers, acquaintances, business associates coming and going, mostly going. In the end, you are alone; you are the monarch of all you survey; and if all you survey is ruination, that's okay, you are the king of the ruins.

What annoys old people is seeing young people ruin their lives in precisely the same way they did.

First of all, he is a nobody; ten years later, he is a voice in the wilderness; ten years later, he is the up-and-comer; ten years later, he is the great and wonderful leader; ten years later, he is the grand old man; ten years later, the books start to come out, telling you what a stupid s.o.b. he was.

The seven ages of man – spills, drills, thrills, bills, ills, pills, wills.

When you are young you try to find some meaning in the chaos around you. Later on you learn that the chaos itself is the meaning.

Until you are about forty, you think you have been unlucky in life, you drew a bad ticket. After that, you find out that everybody drew a bad ticket.

It is the same path we all have to travel. You had to be as foolish as you were to be as wise as you are, as weak as you were to be as strong as you are, as miserable as you were to be as happy as you are, as annoying as you were to be as agreeable as you are.

I've made all sorts of wrong decisions; I'm the kind of guy who only said no once, and then he didn't hear the question properly.

When you look back on your life, you are shamed by all those unworthy actions. But cheer up, they were probably worthy of you at the time you performed them. That they seem unworthy of you now means you have improved; you are approaching that perfection of character which comes on the deathbed.

We are proud of our wisdom, such as it may be, but ashamed of the mistakes which gave it to us.

It's wise to learn from the mistakes of others; you can't live long enough to make them all yourself.

The follies we have committed in the past give us the wisdom and experience to enjoy the follies we commit in the present.

By the time a man is wise enough to give advice, he is too wise to do it.

Too late – ah yes, that is the most interesting and exciting time; that is when you realize the truth about things and people.

Having gone through all the other illusions, one eventually comes to the illusion of being disillusioned.

Life is a rather bad play, in which you are the hero or heroine for a while, then a supporting character, then a minor one, then an extra, following which you sit in the third row back, thinking it is a rather bad play.

I come increasingly to think that the best way to live is in silence, in simplicity – being involved as little as possible with as few people as possible, just watching the show and happy you are no longer on stage.

Life is an obstacle race; the course is some seventy years in length, and nobody wins.

Once you have mastered the rules of the game, the game is nearly ended. Next!

Death may be noble, but the business of dying is squalid.

We spend our lives worrying that someone will take our possessions away from us. God laughs and takes us away from them.

Odds & Ends

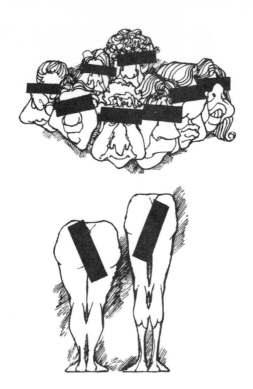

Our Daily Bread

Couldn't life itself be described as a dead-end job?

My first job was a meaningful one. It involved a meaningful barn, a meaningful bucket, and the meaningful end of a cow.

Every job is meaningful. If it only means that you get to eat three times a day, most of the people in this world would settle for it.

One secret of happiness in life is always to have some work left over at the end of the day.

"It's Friday, thank God" – people who say this will end up saying, "It's death, thank God." If working and learning are things that you simply want to get through, then so is living.

I deem myself lucky. I can go to work every day of the year, and there is always work for me to go to.

Happy is the man who is too busy to figure out if he is happy or not.

Management used to be grateful if you worked hard. Then it was grateful if you worked at all. Now it is grateful if you even show up.

An executive is a man who knows how to delegate responsibility – and how to straighten out the disasters that result from such delegation.

A good executive takes the blame upon himself when things go wrong and gives the credit to his staff when things go right.

Efficiency – turning the pile of junk on top of your desk into a pile of junk on top of someone else's desk.

What are the two great dangers to the businessman's health? You might say tobacco and alcohol. I would say lunch and dinner.

Give a man more than he can do, and he will do it; give him less than he can do, and he won't even do that.

Broad is the smile on the face of the tavern keeper when the workingman gets more time off to spend with his family.

When I see the way most people spend their Sunday afternoons, I thank God that I have an office where I can go and work.

At nights, on Saturdays, on Sundays, and on statutory holidays, Lady Luck wanders around looking for men who are still in their stores and offices.

Four men were sent on an identical mission. One couldn't make it because his car broke down. Another couldn't make it because he became ill. Another couldn't make it because he'd been held up and robbed. The fourth returned and said, "Mission accomplished." Later on, it came out that his car had broken down, that he'd been ill, and that he was held up and robbed.

If you habitually show up for work early, you are anxious; you need help. If you habitually show up late, you are hostile; you need help. If you habitually show up on time, you are compulsive; you need help.

You see no future in your job, so you get another one, then submit your resignation. This is the point at which the management calls you in, says it is sorry you are going, and reveals what great plans it had in mind for you.

It is much easier to make people fight for their country than to make them work for it. But, of course, human beings have always preferred fighting to working.

I have decided over a lifetime that human beings have only one right – the right to work. I didn't say the right to a pay cheque, but the right to work, which carries with it the duty to do the work as well and honestly as they possibly can.

A man earns the right to eat not from having a belly, but from doing work that puts food into it.

People who make claim to rights don't deserve them. Men who are men, women who are women, earn their rights every day by their work, their character, and their conduct.

We may eventually forgive the immigrant who goes on welfare, but we will never forgive the one who works harder, or for less, than we do.

It used to be that employers gave preference to younger people – figured they could get more work out of them. Well, that is how it used to be.

When a city is struck with a blizzard, the people under forty phone in to say they can't make it to work. Their calls are taken by the people over forty.

A fair wage is what you pay, an unfair wage is what you get; a fair price is what you charge, an unfair price is what the other fellow charges.

Canadian workers are hideously exploited; they are paid in money.

A union that really wanted to help its members would demand they get their wages not in play money, such as Canadian and American dollars, but in real money, such as gold, German marks, or Swiss francs which are backed by gold.

If a job is so simple that a kid would be happy to do it for $10 a week, you will find a grown man doing it unhappily for $200 a week.

The guy who makes $150 a week would far sooner see all men, including himself, making $125 a week than see some of them making $250 a week.

I remember when Canadians were so proud that they would

rather take a low-pay job than go on welfare. Now they are so proud that they would rather go on welfare than take a low-pay job.

Success to me is having some food in your belly, some clothes on your back, and enjoying whatever sort of life you happen to lead, whether you are making $50 a week or $5,000. Just to be alive, that's success.

Leaning on Learning

What is the purpose of education? My answer would be that after the bus driver has completed his run to Winnipeg, he settles down to read Gibbon's *Decline and Fall*, particularly savouring the naughty parts in Latin.

Canada's universities offer many interesting choices, the best of which is going to work instead.

Famous last words: "Sure, those schools and colleges are costing us a lot of money, but just think of the highly skilled, highly motivated employees we'll be getting out of them."

Education makes a difference. Without it, you are likely to end up digging ditches. With it, you are likely to end up sweeping streets.

Higher education – ah yes, that is what teaches you to clinch the argument by calling your opponent a fascist.

For a well rounded education, you could try curling up with good books and bad librarians.

I love libraries, but I will be damned if I will ever walk into a "Resource Centre."

Ben Franklin told of a man who was so learned that he could name a horse in nine languages and so ignorant that he bought a cow to ride on. They are still around, Ben; we call them B.A.'s.

They have at last achieved equality in the U.S. school system; both blacks and whites are coming out of it illiterate.

Those who can, do; those who can't, get diplomas saying they can.

We should try to get our money's worth out of the schools. It's ridiculous having them stand idle twelve months of the year.

On Being Canadian

There are two possible reasons for a Canadian knowing little or nothing about this country's history and geography: (1) that he wasn't born and brought up here and (2) that he was.

A Canadian is a man who complains because he can't find a parking place right in front of Vic Tanny's.

Bilingualism has some strange results. I heard of an elderly lady who always asks her grocer for Old Fort cheese.

If the environmentalists had been with us a century ago, the Canadian Pacific Railway would now be approaching Thunder Bay.

Canada is a country where mothers take their daughters to the ballet, and fathers take their sons to the hockey game.

I think I would be happy in a country that never changed the design of its stamps.

I am sure Canada will perform valiantly in the next war, providing it is given at least five years advance notice.

God is Alive and Well

People ask me if I believe in God, to which I have to reply, "I notice the sun rose this morning. Did you yourself do anything to bring this about?"

One goldfish told the other, "Of course, there is a God. Who do you think changes the water?"

The audience loves the symphony for what it is; the composer hates it for what it might have been. This is true, I think, in all the creative arts. What the public regards as a masterpiece, the painter or writer or sculptor regards as a fiasco or, at best, as the second-rate expression of a first-rate idea. Only God looked upon His creation and found it good; perhaps He wasn't seeing too well that day.

The sun rises every morning in the East and sets every evening in the West – still another instance of God's compulsion to over-simplify.

Those who place their trust in God wind up less embittered than those who place their trust in man.

We are saved in the next world by our faith; in this one, by our lack of it.

So you don't live up to other people's expectations? Cheer up, neither does God.

If God had meant men to fly, He'd have given them warm beer in a plastic glass.

Grace shouldn't be said before the meal, but after it. One could then decide whether it warranted a long grace, a short grace, or a string of profanities.

Downtown Toronto is mentioned in the Bible (Isaiah 4:1): "In that day seven women shall take hold of one man."

An atheist is a man who has a blind, unreasoning faith that the sun will rise tomorrow morning.

People of different religions can get along pretty well, providing they aren't religious.

Jesus told us to love one another, but that's not easy when so many people (me, for example) are so unlovable. The solution might be to love those whom you can, like those whom you can, and be polite to the rest.

A mother tells me that she has a good son and a naughty one. She fights with the good son all the time, because she expects so much more of him than she does of the naughty one. I wonder if this isn't true in adult life. If you are a bad person, your evil deeds are more or less forgiven – "Oh well, what did you expect from him?" If, on the other hand, you are an honest and kind and reliable person, others expect you to measure up to yourself all the time, indeed to improve on yourself, and they castigate you for your occasional lapses. Would it be irreverent to imagine that Christ was crucified, not for being so good, but for failing to be even better? The mob expected nothing from Barabbas, so he was the one they set free.

Don't worry over all the sins and crimes and blunders you have committed; you may have done some good things and will possibly do some more. Bear in mind the soldier who went to church for the first time and heard the minister read out the Ten Commandments and went down the steps afterwards saying, "Well, at least I never made any graven images."

Heaven is where you are rewarded for the kind deeds which made your earthly life a hell.

God punishes us mildly by ignoring our prayers and severely by answering them.

God is merciful. He has given us four billion other people whom we can blame for our own mistakes and shortcomings.

Do's and Don'ts

If you have good manners, you can get away with almost any kind of morals.

Good, when accompanied by superior force, invariably puts evil to rout.

If Diogenes went looking for an honest man today, someone would steal his lantern.

An honourable man is so mortified by the thought of breaking a promise that he rarely makes any.

It is easier to be honest than to persuade others you are.

Any simpleton can be honest. What counts for much more in this world is to give the appearance of honesty.

Three sure ways to confuse and annoy people – by keeping your word, by telling the truth, by being yourself.

I am never annoyed by half-truths; one is lucky to get even that much.

The explanation that is demanded will probably be a lie. The explanation that is volunteered will probably be a lie, too, but more cheerful, more picturesque.

Any fool can get the facts; getting the truth is something else again.

Truth is a drug so rare, so valuable, so potent, that it should be given only to those who can benefit from it, and in small doses, and occasionally.

Courage, like money, tends to attract the hatred of those who don't have any.

It takes courage to stay in a bad situation and courage to walk out of it. Most people have the staying-in kind of courage, a few have the walking-out kind, and that is the way the world is.

Do your good deeds like a saint; accept your punishment for them like a man.

Common sense, common courtesy, common honesty – why on earth do we use these weird expressions?

When you deal with a stranger, you should assume he is monstrously dishonest until he proves himself ordinarily so.

I work on the principle that every man is a scoundrel until he proves it.

For the Love of Drink

It is a good thing certain restaurants are licenced; by the time the food arrives, you are too drunk to taste it.

At 9:00 A.M., it is easy to decide you will give up drinking; at 9:00 P.M., it is a little more difficult.

A colleague here at the paper mournfully told me, "It's when you stop drinking that you realize why you started."

An alcoholic is a man who drinks more than you do, or who drinks as much as you do, or who drinks somewhat less than you do, but does it more openly.

When a man rages against alcoholism and the terrible damage it does to people, you can be pretty damn sure that he is struggling to cut down his own intake.

An ideal time to speak to a convention audience is at 4:00 P.M. They have gotten over their hangovers from the night before, and they are sober in relation to the night ahead.

I don't object to people who give up smoking and drinking; I just object to them telling me how much better they feel and how much money they are saving.

Pearls of Wisdom

A sensible man knows you can't please everybody; a wise man knows you can't please anybody.

The wise man spends his time trying to put himself in the right; he doesn't waste it by trying to put other people in the wrong.

A wise man will lose as if he expected it and win as if he didn't.

The wise man cheerfully allows himself to be corrected on a

fact or a figure but never corrects other people. That way he retains their goodwill and also makes a profit on the deal.

It is the part of wisdom to keep your word and the part of folly to count on other people keeping theirs.

Every wise man makes provision for possible disasters. Unfortunately, the disasters coming his way are not the ones he made provision for.

That's Life

All my life I have worn short-sleeved shirts, and all my life people have given me cufflinks.

I could draw up statistics to prove that eating, drinking, breathing, walking, and talking are invariably fatal.

Whatever you are doing right now, you had better enjoy it, because you will soon be looking back on it as utter folly.

Being there is the next best thing to calling long distance.

If a human being were as hostile as your average coathanger, he would have to be put away.

Cigarette smokers have a sixth sense which tells them they have got one going somewhere, and they had better find it before it burns the place down.

Supermarkets are great. It takes you twenty seconds to find the item you want and twenty minutes to get out of the place with it.

Time solves every problem and, in the process, adds a couple of new ones.

If the problem has no solution, it isn't a problem; it is just a fact of life, like many others. If the problem has a solution, it isn't a problem either; the problem is the lack of courage and will to adopt the solution.

Life is a series of rehearsals for the gala performance which is always about to take place, but never does.

Life is a tragedy in which the hero keeps fluffing his lines, the heroine has a stuck zipper, and the audience is rooting for the villain.

Don't allow other people to mess up your life; you will have much more fun doing the job yourself.

How great it would be if human existence could be video-taped in advance! Unfortunately, it has to be done live.

Exercise is like life; if it doesn't hurt, it's not doing you any good.

Don't give orders to life; it isn't Room Service; it will bring what it wants, not what you want. PS So will Room Service.

Considering how difficult it is to get through just one day, it is amazing that so many of us manage to get through a lifetime.

Life is an expressway on which the exits and the interchanges are so poorly marked that by the time you see them, it is too late.

I am an optimist; knowing things must get worse before they get better, I cheerfully watch them get worse.

One of my favourite novels in English is Herman Melville's *Moby Dick*. It has no sex or love interest, the hero is a psychotic, the villain is a fish, and everybody comes to a bad end.

Illustrations by Ed Franklin
Design & production by David Shaw
Typesetting by The London Free Press
Printed & bound in Canada
by T. H. Best Printing Company Limited